THE
SMARTER
SCREEN

THE SMARTER SCREEN

SURPRISING WAYS TO INFLUENCE
AND IMPROVE ONLINE BEHAVIOR

SHLOMO BENARTZI

WITH JONAH LEHRER

PORTFOLIO / PENGUIN

PORTFOLIO / PENGUIN

An imprint of Penguin Random House LLC

375 Hudson Street

New York, New York 10014

penguin.com

ISBN 978-1-59184-786-1

Printed in the United States of America

1   3   5   7   9   10   8   6   4   2

Set in Janson Text LT Std

Designed by Alissa Rose Theodor

CONTENTS

ACKNOWLEDGMENTS

This book would not exist without the help of many people. I benefited from huge amounts of feedback, both during the development of the ideas in this book and during the writing process. First, I was incredibly fortunate to get access to many brilliant academics, scientists, and colleagues, who were kind enough to read various drafts of the chapters and offer their insights and comments. I'm very grateful to Peter Ayton, Maya Bar-Hillel, Tibor Besedes, Saurabh Bhargava, Barbara Fasolo, Gavan Fitzsimons, Craig Fox, Dan Goldstein, Noah Goldstein, Michael Hallsworth, David Halpern, Hal Hershfield, Eric Johnson, Yaron Levi, George Loewenstein, Katy Milkman, Daniel Oppenheimer, Katharina Reinecke, Elena Reutskaja, and Philip Tetlock.

A few friends deserve special mention, as they devoted many hours to the book and improved it in countless ways. If it weren't for David Faro, John Payne, and Richard Thaler, *The Smarter Screen* would be far less smart.

I was also lucky enough to get valuable input from many friends in the industry. A big thank you to David Collyer, Udo Frank, Bill Harris, Thomas MacNeil, Charlie Nelson, Cathy Smith, and Matt

Stewart. Danny Kalish read every chapter, often more than once, and offered many important insights that led me in new directions.

It was crucial to me that this book be as accurate as possible. Steve Shu, my very good friend, spearheaded the fact-checking process. In addition, I'm very grateful for the time and diligence of Jolie Martin, Amit Runchal, Namika Sagara, and Hadas Sella. They combed through every citation and double-checked every fact and quote. All remaining mistakes are my own.

This book was guided by a skilled team at Portfolio. I owe a big thank you to Adrian Zackheim for seeing the potential in a book about behavioral economics in the digital age. And my editor, Niki Papadopoulos, helped ensure the book was as readable and engaging as possible.

I want to thank my collaborator, Jonah Lehrer, an amazing friend and brilliant writer. We had a great time working on this book together. It could never have been written without him.

Last, but definitely not least, I want to thank my family. Shalom, my dad, and Leah, my mom, for everything they taught me. My wife, Lesli, and Maya, my little girl, put up with many late nights and countless discussions about the material in this book. They inspire me every day.

INTRODUCTION

On October 1, 2013, the United States government launched a new Web site, www.healthcare.gov, that was designed to help people choose health insurance. In essence, the site was a shopping portal, allowing consumers to compare prices and features on all of the insurance plans available in their local area. Because the government hoped to sign up millions of uninsured Americans, they decided to rely on the scale of the Web.

While most of the media coverage of the Web site centered around its glaring technical glitches, very little attention was paid to a potentially far more important issue: Did the Web site actually help consumers find the best insurance plans? Given the reach of Obamacare, even seemingly minor design details could have a huge impact, influencing a key financial decision in the lives of millions of Americans.

Unfortunately, research suggests that most people probably made poor insurance choices on the Web site. A study conducted by Saurabh Bhargava, George Loewenstein, and me demonstrated that the typical subject using a simulated version of healthcare.gov chose a plan that was $888 more expensive than it needed to be.[1] This was equivalent to roughly 3 percent of their income. Meanwhile, an earlier study, led by Eric Johnson at Columbia University, found that giving consumers more health care options on sites like healthcare .gov dramatically decreased their ability to find the best plan. In fact, even offering people a modest degree of choice meant that nearly 80 percent of them picked suboptimally.[2]

Can this problem be fixed? The online world offers us more alternatives than ever before: the average visitor to healthcare.gov was offered *forty-seven* different insurance plans,[3] while Zappos.com features more than twenty-five thousand women's shoes. But how should Web sites help us choose better?

On the morning of February 21, 2010, an American Predator drone began tracking a pickup truck and two SUVs traveling on a road near the village of Shahidi Hassas in southern Afghanistan. As the drone followed the vehicles, it beamed a live video feed to a crew of analysts based at Creech Air Force Base outside Las Vegas.[4]

Such intelligence is now a staple of modern warfare. The CIA used drones to gather intel on Osama bin Laden's hideout; the Israeli Defense Forces flew dozens of unmanned aircraft over Gaza during the recent conflict; the United States Air Force accumulated more than five hundred hours of aerial video footage *every single day* in Afghanistan and Iraq.[5]

This flood of information creates an obvious problem: someone has to process it. Unfortunately, the evidence suggests that drone crews are often overwhelmed by the visual data. One study, led by Ryan McKendrick at George Mason University, showed that people simulating the multitasking environment of drone operators performed worse on an air defense task;[6] another experiment, which looked at gunners in armored vehicles, found that the soldiers failed to perform their primary task effectively—noticing the bad guys—when a second task was added to the list.[7] In experiment after experiment, the surplus of digital information creates blind spots on the screen.[8]

That's what happened to the analysts tracking those vehicles in southern Afghanistan. According to an internal military investigation,[9] the cubicle warriors in Nevada couldn't handle all of the available information as they toggled back and forth among the video feed, radio chatter, and numerous instant messages. As a result, they failed to notice that the truck and SUVs were actually filled with civilians. And so the drone operators gave the order to fire, unleashing a barrage of Hellfire missiles and rockets. Twenty-three innocent people were killed in the attack.

How can we make such tragedies less likely to happen? What should the Air Force and CIA do to minimize the risk of blind spots on screens? And how can other organizations, from financial institutions to hospitals, deal with the same problem of digital information overload?

On December 14, 2013, Jessica Seinfeld used the Uber app to drop her children off across town at a bar mitzvah and a sleepover.[10] Unfortunately, the ride took place in the midst of a New York City snowstorm, which meant that Uber had put surge pricing into effect. (When demand for drivers is high—say, during a blizzard, or on New Year's Eve—Uber systematically raises its rates to entice more drivers to enter the marketplace.) During this storm, demand for drivers was so high that some Manhattan customers were charged 8.25 times the normal fare. Although Uber warned its customers about the surcharge before they ordered a ride, the warning clearly wasn't effective, as social media soon lit up with complaints of price gouging. Jessica

Seinfeld, for instance, posted a picture of her $415 Uber bill on Instagram, while many others lamented their crosstown rides that cost more than $150.[11] Uber had provided a valuable service—helping people get home in a bad storm—but had also angered a lot of customers. It's never a good sign when your company is the reason people are tweeting the hashtag #neveragain.

The surge pricing problem is indicative of a more common digital hazard, which is that people often think very fast on screens. Uber customers, of course, benefit from this quick pace, as the streamlined app makes it easy for people to book rides with a few taps of the thumb. However, when surge pricing is in effect that same effortless ease can backfire, since consumers book rides on their phone without realizing how much the rides are going to cost.

How should Uber fix its app? Is there any way to help consumers avoid online decisions they'll soon regret?

These three stories illustrate a few of the many ways in which the digital revolution is changing the way we live, from the analysis of military intelligence to the booking of taxi rides. They reveal an age in which we have more information and choices than ever before, and are able to act on them with breathtaking speed. But these stories are also a reminder of the profound challenges that remain. We have more choices, but we choose the wrong thing. We have more information, but we somehow miss the most relevant details. We can act quickly, but that often means we act without thinking.

It's a cliché to complain about these trends. It's easy to lament all the ways the online world leaves us confused and distracted, forgetful and frazzled.

This book is not about those complaints. It is not about how smartphones make us stupid. It is not a requiem for some predigital paradise.

Instead, this book is about how screens can be designed to make us smarter. It's a book of behavioral solutions and practical tools that can improve our digital lives. It's about how the same technological trends that lead people to buy the wrong insurance plan and book a $415 taxi ride can be turned into powerful digital opportunities, rooted in the latest research about how we think and choose on smartphones, tablets, and computers.

Here are three examples of potential solutions. If you want to encourage people to select the best health care plan, or choose the right product on your Web site, then you might want to consider a choice tournament modeled on Wimbledon and March Madness. (Instead of giving people all the options at once, you divide the best options into different rounds—work led by Tibor Besedes shows this dramatically improves decision making.)[12]

And if you want to help intelligence analysts avoid blind spots, it's often helpful to zoom out and provide fewer details about the scene. (In a real-world study conducted in Israel, providing less detailed feedback led to big improvements in decision making among investors.[13] I bet it would also help drone operators.) This fix is not just about giving people less information—it's also about using new information compression technologies to help us cope with our limited attention.

Finally, companies like Uber can do a better job of educating their customers—and thus avoiding a mob of angry ones—by carefully deploying ugly fonts on their Web sites and apps.[14] (This runs counter to the common belief that information should always be as easy to process as possible.) The same approach can also be used to close the digital reading gap, as many studies suggest that we read significantly worse on screens than we do on paper.[15]

These are just a few suggestions for how businesses and governments can use the tools and tactics of behavioral science to improve our online behavior. This book is filled with many more examples, as I believe we are on the cusp of a huge opportunity: By taking advantage of this practical research, we can dramatically boost the quality of our digital decisions. We can see better, learn more, and regret less.

So why am I, a behavioral economist, writing this book? I have devoted my career to studying the mistakes people make so that we might learn to avoid them. For example, in my research with Richard Thaler, a behavioral economist and coauthor of the book *Nudge*,[16] we used psychological insights to help four million employees significantly boost their savings rates using the Save More Tomorrow program.[17] That's the good news. The bad news is that it took us fifteen years to reach that many people. What's worse, there are still tens of millions of Americans whom we failed to help, and who still aren't saving enough. I have been continually frustrated by the slow pace of this process.

My hope is that we can use the scale of technology to bring more fixes to more people in far less time. After all, if you want to influence citizens and customers in the twenty-first century, you don't have to knock on their doors, or interrupt them on the street—you can just interact with them online, using the reach of the digital world to quickly contact vast numbers of people with minimal effort. In fact, influencing behavior on screens can be so efficient and effective that I believe we have a chance to help a billion people think smarter and choose wiser. That's right: *billion*. With a *b*.

However, this opportunity comes with an important caveat: in order to take advantage of these digital nudges, I believe we need to tailor them for our new online environment. Although we like to pretend that our brain isn't altered by technology, new evidence suggests that these splendid inventions are shifting the patterns of our behavior in all sorts of subtle ways. What's more, these shifts are often predictable, allowing us to anticipate how people will act on a device, and how they will respond to our interventions. (We can even explain some consistent quirks of digital behavior, such as why people value items more when shopping on a tablet,[18] or why they will probably get lower scores when taking the SAT on a computer,[19] or why they order pizza with more calories when ordering off a Web site.[20]) The end result is that we need to update our behavioral toolkit for the digital age. This book will give you the tools you need now, at least if you want to nudge people the right way on screens.

Let me be clear: I'm not saying your head has been rewired by your smartphone. (Human nature evolved over millions of years; it's unlikely to be transformed in a decade or two.) Nevertheless, there are many relevant differences in offline versus online thinking, which should be reflected in the designs of our screens. And since every business is now a digital business, and nearly every consumer is making important decisions on their gadgets, it's incredibly important that we get these designs right. The medium of information and decision making has changed. So should our interventions and nudges.

Of course, this is all very new research, which means that a few disclaimers are in order. Some of the studies in this book directly compare online and offline behavior, while other studies are more suggestive. When the evidence is more speculative, I will make that clear. In addition, these behavioral tools won't be able to solve every digital problem. While we can design screens that might make it easier to deal with information overload and choose better insurance, we're not going to completely eliminate online mistakes or mollify every upset Uber customer.

Technological revolutions provide us with a rare opportunity to fundamentally reimagine how we think and live. Who could have guessed that, one day, many of the most important military decisions would be made on a computer? Or that the layout of a Web site would determine how many millions of Americans will get health care insurance and 401(k) accounts? Or that the smartphone would be the last thing most of us see at night and the first thing we see in the morning?

We are living in a world increasingly made of zeros and ones; more and more of our lives are taking place on screens. This book helps us take advantage of this moment, ensuring that we won't squander the possibilities of the digital revolution.

Let's get started.

CHAPTER 1

———

The Mental Screen

THE FOURTH NIGHT

I'd like to begin with a story. It's a story that takes place in a time before the Internet, way back in the early 1990s. The story involves a man who wants to book a hotel room in Cleveland. (Great story, huh?) There are a few different ways this booking could happen.

Perhaps the man has a trusted travel agent, and so he calls the agent and tells her what he'd like: a nice three-star hotel, close to the airport. She takes down his preferences, checks her paper files, and then picks up the phone to call the hotel. For her services, she charges the hotel a 10 percent commission.

Alternatively, our intrepid traveler might want to book the room himself. If that's the case, and if he's never been to Cleveland before, then he needs a travel guide. A tourist manual. Maybe it's *Fodor's*, or *Let's Go*, or the newsprint manuals provided at the local AAA office—there's no booking without a book.

Fast-forward to the present day. Chances are, our protagonist now relies on the Internet to make his hotel reservations. (The number of travel agents employed by travel agencies has declined by roughly 55 percent in the last fifteen years.)[1] He almost certainly begins with Google, searching for a hotel near the Cleveland airport. A few milliseconds later, his screen is filled with results.

If you look closely at the screen, however, you'll notice something strange, as the top results don't refer our traveler to actual hotel Web sites. Instead, they send him to a category of Web sites called online travel agents, or OTAs, which have come to dominate the market for hotel reservations. Think here of Booking.com, Kayak, Expedia, or Hotels.com. These sites don't run hotels or own hotels. They are a middleman, pure and simple, just like human travel agents. All they do is lift photographs and relevant information from hotel Web sites and then organize the listings based on a customer's preferences. Do you care about location? Price? Star ratings? Pool? A free shuttle to the airport?

Here's a question: Can you guess how much OTAs charge for commission? Keep in mind that OTAs are primarily aggregators, helping customers search through all the hotels in a given area. While hotel owners have to buy the land, build the hotel, and then pay a large staff to take care of the customers and property, OTAs have none of these expenses. Instead, their costs are dominated by digital advertising, as they seek out ways to grab your attention on a digital device. Of course, once they've got your attention—after they secure your gaze and clicks—OTAs can then sell that attention back to the hotels.

So how much do you think your attention is worth? What sort of commission can OTAs get away with charging hotel owners for each booking?

My initial guess was 5 percent, although even that might seem a little high. Human travel agents, after all, have to deal directly with their customers. They need to spend time learning their preferences and finding a suitable hotel. On average, all of this work gets them only a 10 percent commission. OTAs, on the other hand, rely on algorithms to do all the work—no personal touch is required. It seems like a clear example of the online world *lowering* the cost of business, squeezing out the human middlemen and making the world a more efficient place.

But I was wrong. In fact, I was off by a factor of five. Because here's the shocking truth: OTAs routinely charge commissions between 20 and 30 percent.[2] Think, for a moment, about how remarkable this is—when you book a hotel through Expedia or Priceline or Travelocity, one out of every four nights goes to the Web site. They haven't changed the sheets, or heated the pool, or restocked the minibar. They don't pay the mortgage or the staff. And yet, they are taking a fourth of hotel revenues.

How do OTAs get away with this? Why would hotels ever pay such exorbitant commissions to booking Web sites, especially when their own Web sites offer the exact same services?

The answer reveals a very interesting truth about life in the twenty-first century. The extremely lucrative business model of the OTAs is based on taking advantage of the mismatch between all of the information on our physical screens—these digital displays we spend all day staring at—and our *mental screen*, which is the information we can actually pay attention to. The high commissions of these Web sites might seem ridiculous, but they have identified an opportunity to help people think and choose better online. The point of this book is that such opportunities are everywhere.

But only if you know how to find them.

THE FIRE HOSE

Before the Internet was in your pocket, the challenge of booking a hotel was finding useful information. It wasn't easy to get the phone number, let alone some relevant pictures of the guest rooms. We were choosing in the dark, which is why we were so reliant on travel agents to make the choice for us.

But now? We are drowning in information. A simple Google search for "Cleveland airport hotel" returns more than five million hits.[3] And even if we browse the first few pages of results, there's still the problem of making a selection. Should we stick with the Holiday Inn? Is the Sheraton worth the extra money? Because there's no clear answer, we end up perusing the Web sites, comparing pictures, searching for relevant details. We read way too many user reviews. It's an arduous process, sure to leave us longing for the days of travel agents.

Needless to say, the surfeit of Google results for a Cleveland hotel is only a tiny example of the profound changes unleashed by the information revolution. Here's a metaphor that has helped me think about the information age. Like all metaphors, it's an imperfect comparison—it probably *underestimates* the magnitude of the change we're living through—but I think it helps us grasp the tradeoffs triggered by the digital revolution. Once upon a time, the flow of data was more like the drip of water from a leaky fixture. In fact, the amount of information was so minuscule that most people were thirsty for more; we had excess attentional capacity. But then along came Gutenberg, print culture took off, and, by the middle of the twentieth century, the flow of information was more like the steady stream of water coming out of a kitchen faucet.

Computers changed everything. Starting in the 1980s, the quantity of information began to rise at an exponential pace. If the information in every letter delivered by the U.S. Postal Service in 2010 were added up, the amount would be roughly equal to five petabytes.[4] Google processes that much data on a slow afternoon. (According to a recent estimate from IBM data scientists, "90 percent of all the data in the world today has been created in the last two years.")[5] The situation is just as extreme if you look at out personal interactions. According to a study by Martin Hilbert, the quantity of two-way communication done by people daily—that includes phone conversations, e-mail, and text—has gone from the equivalent of two newspaper pages in 1986 to twenty entire newspapers in 2010.[6] It's as if our kitchen faucet was replaced by the highest-pressure fire hose, spraying us in the face with a deluge of data.

The point of the fire hose metaphor is that the presence of more water—a fire hose sprays approximately 125 times more gallons per minute than a kitchen faucet—doesn't translate into increased drinking capacity. (In fact, it might even lead to less drinking, as we'll see shortly.) That's because the human mouth has fixed constraints, and can only open so wide. It doesn't matter how much water is flowing by our face—we will never be able to gulp more than a few ounces at a time.

The human mind is the same way. When it comes to how much information we can process, the limiting factor is rarely what's on the screen, for the amount of information on the monitor will almost always exceed the capacity of the mind to take it in. Instead, we are limited by the scarcity of attention, by our inability to focus on more than a few things at the same time.

Herbert Simon, a Nobel Prize–winning psychologist, was one of the first people to understand this. In 1971, back when the information age was just beginning, Simon realized that the growth of information would have massive psychological consequences. "In an information-rich world, the wealth of information means a dearth of something else: a scarcity of whatever it is that information consumes," he wrote.[7] For Simon, what information consumed was "rather obvious: it consumes the attention of its recipients." Furthermore, because attention is a relatively inelastic property—the mind can notice only so many things at once—"a wealth of information creates a poverty of attention," forcing people to make difficult choices about what to perceive and think about.

Although Simon's quote is now a catchphrase—there's lots of talk about our "attention economy"—Simon wrote those lines before computers were commonplace. He was worried about information overload before there was e-mail, or Google, or smartphones, or the Apple Watch. Back when newspapers didn't refresh their headlines every five minutes. In other words, what Simon considered "a wealth of information" would now feel like a data desert. This means, of course, that the relationship between information and attention has only gotten more extreme. It is a behavioral principle—too much information leads to a scarcity of attention—that's amplified on screens.

The ironic takeaway is that, in the age of information, we are less able than ever before to process information, since our attention is all used up. (To return to our fire hose metaphor: we are drenched in water, but thirstier than ever.) If you want some evidence of our collective attention deficit, consider what happens when you give people a short test to make sure they're paying attention. Such "attention filters" are a standard protocol of social science conducted on screens, a way to make sure that subjects are actually reading the text and following instructions. (In my research, I exclude subjects who fail the filter.) Here, for instance, is a slightly modified version of the attention filter pioneered by Daniel Oppenheimer and colleagues in a 2009 paper.[8] Please read the text and follow the instructions:

> *Most modern theories of decision making recognize the fact that decisions do not take place in a vacuum. Individual preferences and knowledge, along with situational variables, can greatly impact the decision process. In order to facilitate our research on decision making we are interested in knowing certain factors about you, the decision maker. Specifically, we are interested in whether you actually take the time to read the directions; if not, then some of our questions will be unclear. So, in order to demonstrate that you have read the instructions, please do not answer any of the questions on the next page. You will begin answering questions again on the following page.*

When I eat out I like to try the most unusual items the restaurant serves, even if I am not sure I would like them.

__ Agree

__ Somewhat Agree

__ Somewhat Disagree

__ Disagree

It's a trick question, of course: if you answered it, then you clearly didn't pay enough attention to the instructions.

So how many people fail the filter? The results are consistently depressing. When Oppenheimer and colleagues gave 480 subjects a version of the attention filter with pen and paper, anywhere between 14 and 28.7 percent of them failed the test, depending on their level of motivation. However, when the scientists gave a similar attention filter to 213 people on a computer screen, they got a much higher failure rate of 46 percent. In one instance, the scientists could replicate the results of classic behavioral science experiments on a computer only if they disregarded those who failed the attention filter. We are a scatterbrained species, especially when thinking on screens.

Let's pause, for a moment, to consider the implications of this finding. How many surveys have you filled out on a screen? How many questions have you been asked? I'm guessing the answer is a lot. The attention filter data, of course, suggests that a near majority of the responses come from people who aren't paying attention. Their answers aren't that useful because they didn't take the time to read the questions.

And this brings us back to the exorbitant commissions of OTAs. The Web sites realize that we are probably overwhelmed with

16

information and options. They know we don't want to scroll through a chaotic list of Google results, or take the time to visit each hotel Web site. And so they make it simple for us: they buy up all the ads at the top of the search results. Try it: Search for any hotel in any city and I guarantee that the top paid result will be an OTA. Booking .com, for instance, is one of the largest spenders on Google, paying $7.68 for every click on a "new york hotel" ad.[9] Once we click on an OTA link, the goal of the Web site is to rank our surfeit of travel options based on the one or two variables we think are most important. In short, they are sites for people who feel overwhelmed, who don't know how to cope with the fire hose of travel information, or who don't have any idea what to do with five million hits after searching for Cleveland airport hotels.

That certainly sounds nice—I often find OTAs quite useful— but it still doesn't answer the deeper mystery, which is how OTAs get away with taking every fourth night as a commission. To answer that question, one needs to remember a basic lesson of macroeconomics, which is that money chases scarcity. That's why diamonds are more valuable than gold, and gold is more valuable than quartz. It's why the price of any resource—and it doesn't matter if the resource is plutonium or crude oil—goes up when demand exceeds supply. Fortunes are made from scarcities, and the richest people are those who notice the scarcities first.

So what's scarce in the twenty-first century? It's not hotel rooms in Cleveland. And it's not information about those rooms. Instead, this surplus of possibilities has created a serious scarcity of attention, just as Herbert Simon predicted. OTAs are successful because they help us deal with this scarcity.

The end result is that, in the age of information, established travel brands like InterContinental and Hilton are stuck. They know they are losing lots of money to Booking.com and Expedia and every other OTA. They realize they can't afford to forfeit 25 percent of their revenues indefinitely, which is why they insist that things will change, that consumers will begin going to their sites to reserve a room. (Most hotel chains now offer a "Best Rate Guarantee," assuring customers that they will get the cheapest price if they book directly.) And yet, people continue to rely on OTAs: in late 2013, the market share of OTA hotel bookings underwent a sharp increase, growing at nearly 2.5 times the rate of hotel Web site bookings.[10] If current trends continue, I wouldn't be surprised if OTA commissions exceeded 50 percent in the near future. This would mean, of course, that the majority of a hotel room's price would go to the digital middleman, and that getting your attention would be more valuable than providing you with an actual place to sleep.

The lesson is simple: human attention has become the sweet crude oil of the twenty-first century. If you can control the levers of human attention, then you can essentially charge whatever you'd like.

THE BOUNDED BRAIN

A few months ago, I walked out of a meeting with a good idea. An unusually good idea. One of the best ideas I'd had in months.

But this story is not about that idea. Instead, it's about what happened afterward. I'd just left a meeting in New York City and I was headed back to my hotel. I'd traveled this route countless times before: I knew how to get to the subway station, where to wait for the train, and when to get off.

And yet, on this afternoon, I made an elementary mistake. While my mind was occupied with my great new idea—I was taking some notes on my iPhone—I somehow wandered over to the wrong side of the station. Although I needed the downtown train, I found myself on the uptown platform. Mildly embarrassed, I left the uptown platform, paid for another fare, and resumed thinking about my new idea.

Here's the punchline: I then repeated the *exact same mistake* and found myself, once again, waiting for a train headed in the wrong direction. Because I was so distracted by my new idea, I was forced to buy three subway tickets for the same ride. Not my finest moment.

This is an ordinary failure of cognition. It happens to most of us many times over the course of a day, as we commit small errors while thinking about bigger things. Maybe you're preoccupied with thoughts of lunch, so you misread an e-mail. Or maybe you're paying so much attention to your phone that you walk into a wall, or run a stop sign, or get on the wrong subway train. Because the mind has limited thinking capacity—it can pay attention to only so many things at once—we often fail to notice important details of the world.

One of the first psychologists to investigate these innate mental constraints was George Miller. In an influential paper presented in 1956 at a meeting of the Institute of Radio Engineers at MIT, Miller proposed that the brain was actually a bounded machine, deeply constrained by its short-term memory. The title of a published version of his paper—"The Magical Number Seven, Plus or Minus Two"[11]—says it all, for he insisted that people can remember only about seven pieces of information (+/–2) at any given time. This is why all the relevant numbers in our life, from license plates to phone numbers, are about the same length. If they were any longer, we wouldn't be able to remember them.

Miller's short paper revealed the information processing bottle-necks of the human mind. As the years passed, scientists got better at measuring these bottlenecks, outlining all the ways in which the personal computer inside our head was a bounded device. I wish I could think about big ideas *and* take notes on my phone *and* navigate the New York City subway at the same time, but I can't. And if I want to avoid wasting time and money on extra train tickets in the future, then I should begin by admitting my limitations, knowing that my attention is a more limited resource than I'd like to believe. As we'll soon see, this same mental limitation has critical implica-tions for all sorts of activities, from driving in the digital age to managing patient care.

Here's an exercise known as the reading span task, which was invented in a 1980 paper published by Meredyth Daneman and Patri-cia Carpenter.[12] I'm going to present you with a series of sentences drawn from their task that I'd like you to read aloud. Please try to remember the final word of each sentence. I've **boldfaced** the words to make it a little easier.

- When at last his eyes opened, there was no gleam of triumph, no shade of **anger**.

- The taxi turned up Michigan Avenue where they had a clear view of the **lake**.

- Great things are not done by impulse, but by a series of small things brought **together**.

- One exercise of the mind is the habit of forming clear and precise **ideas**.

- After playing notes and more notes, it is simplicity that emerges as the crowning reward of **art**.

- His parents couldn't understand why he wanted a tattoo on his right **shoulder**.

- The director was very popular, until the employees heard about his **affair**.

Are you done? Now please turn the page.

I'd like you to write down the last word of each sentence in the order in which it was read.

How'd you do? It's a hard test, right? While Miller argued that the capacity of short-term memory was about seven items, the reading span task suggests that it's actually much lower. According to most studies, we're able to remember only three or four of the final words when we read the sentences out loud.[13] And it's not just the reading span task: As psychologists came up with new ways of measuring the amount of information we can attend to—this is known as *working memory*—they discovered that Miller's magical number was way too optimistic. In an influential series of papers, the psychologist Nelson Cowan argued that the true magical number is actually four (plus or minus one), with most tests of working memory showing that we start to miss crucial information whenever the number of bits (letters, words, numbers, colors, whatever) exceeds that amount.[14]

This is a sobering finding. We like to imagine ourselves as Promethean beings; the human brain is supposed to be the most amazing machine in the known universe. But when you start to probe our information processing specs, what you soon discover is that we are defined by our shortcomings. Because we are living in a world overflowing with information, and because the mind can process only such a small amount of it, we are forced to constantly choose what to attend to. It doesn't matter how much data you throw up onto the screen—we can notice only about four bits of it. The rest is noise. Wasted pixels.

The smallness of our magical number has a huge effect on how people make choices. Consider this experiment. You're sitting in a room in a lab. A scientist walks in and says that he's conducting a study of human memory. (He's fibbing—he's actually studying your limited mental bandwidth.) The scientist gives you a seven-digit number to remember, and asks you to walk down the hall to a second room where your memory will be tested. On the way to the testing room, you pass by a refreshment cart for subjects taking part in the experiment. You are given a choice between a slice of chocolate cake with a cherry topping or a bowl of fruit salad. What do you choose?

Now let's replay the experiment. The only difference is that instead of being asked to remember a seven-digit number, you are given only two numbers, a far easier mental task. You then walk down the hall, and are given the same choice between cake and fruit.

You probably don't think the number of digits will affect your choice. But you'd be wrong. When the results from the two different memory groups were tallied up, the scientists observed a striking shift in behavior. Sixty-three percent of people trying to remember seven digits chose the cake, compared with only 41 percent of the two-digit subjects. (The results were even more extreme among subjects who scored high on a measure of impulsivity, with 84 percent choosing cake in the seven-digit condition, compared with only 38 percent in the two-digit condition.)[15]

Why did the two groups behave so differently? According to Baba Shiv, the Stanford scientist who designed the experiment along with Alexander Fedorikhin, it's very difficult to memorize seven random digits—our short-term memory is stretched to the breaking point. Unfortunately, this means that we don't have enough mental resources left over to resist the cake. Instead of thinking about our diet, or the benefits of eating healthy, we think only of immediate gratification, and how good that cake will taste. This is what happens when too much information creates a scarcity of attention—we can pay attention only to what's right in front of our face.

And this isn't just a problem for our waistline. In a 2013 study published in *Science*, a team of psychologists, including Anandi Mani, Sendhil Mullainathan, Eldar Shafir, and Jiaying Zhao, showed that a shortage of cognitive resources can also help explain the poor decision making of those living in poverty.[16] (Studies show that people of lower socioeconomic status, for instance, are less likely to adhere to drug regimens, less likely to show up on time or keep an appointment, less focused at work, and worse at financial planning.)[17] While conventional explanations focus on a lack of education as the root cause—poor people just don't know any better—the scientists focus on "the mental processes required by poverty." They argue that being poor is an all-consuming condition, and that a "preoccupation with pressing budgetary concerns" leaves people with fewer attentional resources to make long-term plans. "Being poor means coping not just with a shortfall of money, but also with a concurrent shortfall of cognitive resources," they write.[18] The scientists estimate that the cognitive impact of poverty is roughly equivalent to losing a full night of sleep or suffering a thirteen-point drop in IQ scores.

These cognitive deficits have serious repercussions. It's long been known, for instance, that low-income people are far less likely to participate in 401(k) plans, which leaves them with a shortage of savings in retirement. While some might speculate that this lack of savings is due to a lack of income—the poor can't spare a dime—it turns out that, if low-income people are automatically enrolled in a savings plan, then the vast majority end up saving for retirement, even though they are free to opt out.[19] This suggests that the issue is not just about money, for the money can be found. Rather, it's also about finding the mental bandwidth to plan for the future.

It's not only the poor who are affected by the bounded nature of the brain. Even the president of the United States has to pay attention to the scarcity of attention. In a recent interview with *Vanity Fair*, President Obama confessed that he wears only gray or blue suits. Why? Because he is always trying to "pare down" his decisions. "I don't want to make decisions about what I'm eating or wearing," Obama said. "Because I have too many other decisions to make."[20] By limiting his fashion and diet options, the president is able to preserve his attention for the more important matters of state.

This brings us back to the digital world. Given the feebleness of our mental capacity—our magical number is probably smaller than the number of fingers on one hand—it's only reasonable to wonder about how the mind is being adversely affected by the excess of information in the twenty-first century. If a few extra numbers are enough to sway us to choose chocolate cake, then how are we affected by a world in which our screens are always alerting us to new e-mails and texts and hyperlinks? (Glenn Wilson, a psychologist at Gresham College, London, found that simply having an unread e-mail in your inbox is so distracting that it reduces your effective IQ score by roughly ten points.)[21] And given our information processing bottlenecks, how are we supposed to deal with an online environment in which the typical Web site contains a multitude of options and hundreds of words? This artificial environment is not the world we evolved to survive in; the technology reveals our weak spots. That's why OTA's have a business model.

And yet, the fundamental problem—this mismatch between the

information displayed and what we can actually process—keeps getting worse.

THE SHRINKING MAGICAL NUMBER

The Department of Veterans Affairs (VA) was an early adopter of electronic medical records. The innovation was born of need, as the VA network of hospitals is so large—the system includes more than 1,700 sites of care, treating more than eight million people every year—that doctors required a way to access a patient's records at different locations.[22] While the development of the system has cost several billion dollars, it's widely credited with improving care and limiting medical mistakes, especially for medication.[23] As part of this ongoing digital update, Veterans Affairs also created a new system designed to automatically inform doctors whenever one of their patients received an abnormal test result. The goal of the new system was to minimize the possibility of a missed result, perhaps because a doctor forgot to follow up, or because a piece of paper got misplaced amid all the files.

At first glance, the digitization of medical results seems like an excellent idea, a clear example of how the online world can help people compensate for their scattered minds. While VA doctors were still responsible for too many patients, at least according to various reports from the inspector general at the Department of Veterans Affairs,[24] this new electronic system was supposed to let them cope, squeezing out a little more efficiency from their overburdened clinics.

Unfortunately, the latest research suggests that these automatically generated "medical alerts" have not solved the problem of missed test results. Why not? *Because there are way too many of them.* According to a detailed analysis led by Dr. Hardeep Singh, the typical primary care doctor working at a VA facility receives more than sixty alerts every day, with 86.9 percent of doctors believing that the quantity of alerts is excessive. Most worrisome, perhaps, is that nearly 70 percent of doctors report "receiving more alerts than they could effectively manage."[25]

Such information overload causes real problems, with nearly a third of doctors admitting that they had personally missed test results that caused delays in care. In a separate study, Singh and his colleagues measured the scope of the problem, concluding that "7 percent of abnormal outpatient laboratory results and 8 percent of abnormal imaging results lacked follow-up within 30 days."[26] This means, of course, that a significant percentage of tests ordered by doctors that come back "abnormal" never get looked at again.

The VA doctors are a cautionary tale. They are a reminder that, at a certain point, the amount of information doesn't just create a scarcity of attention—it actually makes it harder to deploy whatever attention we have left. (As Dr. Clement McDonald noted, in a commentary on the Singh work, "If everything is important, then nothing is.")[27] And that's where technology comes in. The magical number of working memory has always been small. But I'm worried that it's actually getting smaller in the twenty-first century. Think of that fire hose metaphor—if you were actually being sprayed in the face with 250 gallons every minute, I bet you would actually drink *less* than if you had access to an ordinary faucet. The abundance becomes a curse.

This trade-off is easy to understand when it comes to water. However, we often fail to realize that the same trade-offs also apply to the mind, so that an increase in the volume of information can actually lead to less information processing. Perhaps the most common example of this phenomenon comes when we try to multitask while driving. It's probably obvious that texting on the highway is a terrible idea, because our vision is divided between a screen and the road. (That's why forty-four states and the District of Columbia now have texting-while-driving bans in place.)

But what about a hands-free phone conversation? That should be fine, right? Alas, the evidence suggests that even a brief phone conversation can dramatically interfere with our ability to pay attention to the road. In one study of simulated driving led by David Strayer and colleagues at the University of Utah, subjects talking on their phones "missed seeing up to 50 percent of their driving environments, including pedestrians and red lights."[28] (They were also ten times more likely to not stop at a stop sign.)[29] Another experiment by Strayer and colleagues found that people talking on their phones had *slower* reaction times than drivers with a blood alcohol level at the legal limit.[30]

What causes these mental deficits? The scientists blame *inattention blindness*, which occurs whenever the amount of information streaming into the brain exceeds our ability to process it. As a result, the sensory world of these drivers seems to shrink; blind spots appear out of nowhere. And so we run the red light, not because we didn't see it, but because we didn't *notice* it. A routine act has become extremely dangerous, for our attention is all used up. The mind is like an old computer struggling to run a new operating system.

The logic of inattention blindness has clear implications for the online world. It suggests that a screen filled with an excessive amount of information will actually decrease our ability to process it. Just as drivers can't talk and watch the road, so are people easily overwhelmed by all the data streaming out of their electronic gadgets. Take, for instance, a recent study by neuroeconomists at Caltech, which showed that consumers making food choices under a heavy "cognitive load"—

they were given a difficult working memory task—were far more likely to choose items that were easy to perceive, even if they conflicted with their actual food preferences.[31] In other words, they had so little available attention that they failed to select what they actually wanted, and instead settled for whatever they managed to see. The end result was bad decision making.

Is there a solution here? In their work on the cognitive effects of poverty, Anandi Mani and colleagues insist that policy makers should try to avoid "imposing cognitive taxes" on the least well off.[32] We should realize that attention is scarce and getting scarcer, and that even mental tasks that don't seem so onerous—such as filling out a tax form—can actually leave us utterly depleted. This suggests that, whenever possible, the government should dramatically simplify the presentation of information and limit the number of alternatives. Instead of giving poor people a plethora of choices—healthcare.gov offered some people more than 150 alternatives—there should be smart defaults. Forms should be prefilled whenever possible, and people should be sent timely reminders. "Policy-makers should beware of imposing cognitive taxes on the poor just as they avoid monetary taxes on the poor," write Mani and colleagues.

I'm not pretending that I've got all the answers, or that I know how to fix this chronic problem, because I certainly don't. Nevertheless, there are some important changes we can make that will make it easier for people to drink from the fire hose of the twenty-first century.

Take the use of compression. One of George Miller's insights was that the human mind had a clever trick for expanding its attentional bandwidth.[33] Although we could pay attention to only a few bits of information at any given moment, we were also capable of chunking those bits together. My daughter Maya, for instance, likes to play with my iPad. Unfortunately, she had trouble remembering my random numerical passwords. So we came up with the following solution, which works out nicely: my password is now the numbers spelled out by her name (6292). Because the digits conform to a "chunk" she already knows—the letters in her name—it's easy for her to remember the extra information.

While Miller argued that chunking was typically a by-product of experience, it's clear that good design can also help speed up the learning process, just like an effective driving teacher. By exposing the mind to effective shortcuts—by showing us *how* to compress the information—it's possible to accelerate the act of chunking, and thus make us less vulnerable to the limits of attention. Sometimes, this is as simple as relying on visuals to tell a story (a good picture is probably worth more than a thousand words) or dividing a large choice set into useful categories. (We'll look at effective strategies for helping consumers make difficult decisions in chapter 7.)

We should also be more willing to leave information *out*. One of the fundamental insights of OTAs, such as Expedia and Booking .com, is that less is often more, which is why they carefully control the quantity of hotel information on display. Because consumers are so overwhelmed with alternatives, they have to be guided through the decision-making process, provided with easy categories and big buy buttons. Instead of telling them everything, these popular sites encourage people to pick the one variable they care most about— location, price, etc.—and then use that filter to make a choice.

Too many hotel Web sites have yet to learn this lesson. For the most part, the major hotel chains have tried to win back online customers by *adding* features to their Web sites, filling up the screen with even more information. Just look at the Web site of my favorite hotel in London: the Corinthia. The site means well—it provides potential customers with all sorts of seemingly relevant facts, from the square footage of the rooms to whether or not they have a coffee machine inside. There are multiple video tours of the property and an entire section of the Web site devoted to local tourist attractions. These are well-intentioned extras, but every new feature comes with a cost, making the attention of potential customers even scarcer. (I tend to prefer the Corinthia's streamlined mobile Web site, which makes it much easier to find the hotel's phone number and make a reservation.) Of course, when consumers are overwhelmed, they are much more likely to head back to the OTAs, if only because they are designed around the scarcity of our attention.

THE APP DOCTOR

There is a larger lesson here: we need to treat attention as a literal resource. In the twentieth century, people got rich owning real estate and oil wells. In the twenty-first century, however, wealth is generated by those who control attention. This is why, as I write this in late 2014, Apple is the most valuable company in the world according to its market capitalization, having passed ExxonMobil. (Depending on the day, Microsoft is either the second or third most valuable company, followed by Google at number four.) It's why Expedia is worth several billion dollars more than the InterContinental Hotels Group.[34]

So what would happen if we treated attention as a literal resource? I think we'd do a better job of learning to value it. The Internet, after all, is already pretty transparent about the worth of attention. Google gives us free e-mail if we're willing to put up with their targeted ads; Spotify offers a vast music library in exchange for short commercials;

Amazon sells Kindles at a discount if shoppers look at their promotions. In all of these instances, we are bartering with our working memory, trading away the gaze of our eyeballs for discounted gadgets and free online services.

What I want to do is find a way to value our attention for purposes other than advertising dollars. For instance, in a clinical trial currently in progress, a team of researchers at UCLA are giving women smartphones capable of tracking their movement and pinging them with health-related questions, such as whether or not they're eating enough fruits and vegetables. The researchers have reported very promising results, as those women given the phones have shown significant decreases in blood pressure, cholesterol, and levels of stress and anxiety. They've also adopted healthier eating and exercise habits.[35]

I think this study has an obvious extension: we should start giving away free smartphones in exchange for a small allotment of attention from the smartphone user. Perhaps that attention is used to send subjects reminders to live a healthy life, or maybe to avoid risky behaviors. The point is that the messages would have to trigger only small changes in behavior before they paid for that phone. While it would cost roughly $75 billion to buy every worker in the United States a new smartphone—there are roughly 150 million people in the workforce, and a high-end smartphone without a contract costs about $500—that's a much smaller amount than the costs associated with our *un*healthy choices that these new smartphones might help prevent. For instance, according to a recent paper published in the *Annals of Internal Medicine*, patients failing to properly take their medication cost society somewhere between $100 billion and $289 billion *every year*.[36] (It's estimated that nearly 50 percent of prescriptions for chronic diseases are not used as prescribed.)[37] Obesity, meanwhile, adds another $190 billion in direct health care costs. Drunk driving? $114 billion.[38] Smoking? Nearly $290 billion.[39] I'm not saying that a few targeted messages on your smartphone will cure nicotine addiction, or finally make that diet stick. But I do believe that technology can help at the margins, and thus reduce the magnitude of these very costly societal problems. In fact, these problems are so expensive that I wouldn't be surprised if, in the very near future, employers and insurance companies start giving us free smartphones and other gadgets in exchange for the ability to pester us with reminders to make healthier choices. One of the tasks of a doctor, then, would be to also become an app doctor, helping people figure out which digital tools will lead to improved health outcomes for each patient. If we get the incentives right, the smartphone can become a prompt for better living. I don't know about you, but I'd happily put up with a few annoying pings on my phone in exchange for a diet that sticks.

Furthermore, I believe that treating attention like a valued resource would come with a significant ancillary benefit: we could learn how to improve human behavior. Right now, smart corporations are doing most of the learning, primarily through a process known as A/B testing. In essence, A/B testing is a controlled experiment conducted on Web users, in which two different conditions—an A and a B—are shown to a large sample. Then, the behavior of these users is measured, allowing designers to compare the impact of the two conditions. You have unwittingly participated in countless such experiments. It's often said that Google is so reliant on A/B testing—according to *Wired*, the company ran more than seven thousand A/B tests on its search engine in 2011—that one can't use a Google service without being part of an active experiment.[40]

The knowledge gained from all this experimentation is often extremely valuable. Take, for instance, the Web design of OTAs, which has been refined by constant A/B testing. Sometimes, this testing leads to significant insights, even if the changes themselves are relatively simple. When I asked several different OTAs about their biggest "conversion uplifts"—that's tech-speak for screen changes that influence consumer behavior—they invariably mentioned small tweaks to the site, such as increasing the font size of the price or changing the color of the text. Because what you often discover is that small changes can have a big impact on how we think and choose.

I think it's time for a wider variety of institutions and organizations to get into the A/B testing game. I have no problem with Expedia experimenting with its font size, or with Amazon tinkering with its Web site layout, but I hope we also experiment with apps that aim to improve our health or help us save money instead of spend it. In short, if we want to help people make better decisions in the future, then we need to understand the psychology of screens, and how people make choices in an age of too much information and too little working memory. Of course, that sort of practical understanding will require experimentation. It will require lots of A/B tests. It will require giving away phones in exchange for a few seconds of a person's attention, as we try to figure out how to maximize the impact of this precious and scarce mental resource.

Because there is nothing inherently scary about scarcity. In fact, one of the basic premises of economics is that scarcity is an inevitable by-product of progress. As Adam Smith pointed out in *The Wealth of Nations*, nature might be able to satisfy the wants of brutes and animals, but human beings seek constant improvement, which leads to recurring shortages. While Smith associated scarcity with a lack of material resources—during the Industrial Revolution, people needed more coal and wood and land—the most important scarcities of the information age are psychological, and caused by our new abundance of information. Instead of fearing these changes, we should find a way to take advantage of them.

That's where we turn next. Although we will explore many different subjects in this book, from the possibilities of personalization to the problem of excessive choice, one of the recurring themes is the nature of attention. We will look at the accelerated pace of thought on screens—you are evaluating Web sites and apps in a fraction of a second—and tools for slowing the mind down, so that we can remember more of what we read and make better decisions. We will start with the fastest events, those judgments that happen so quickly you don't even know you're making them, and we will end with tools designed to help you pause and reflect on the most important issues in your life. That's our arc—from fast to slow, problem to solution.

ASK YOURSELF

The mismatch between the physical screen and our mental screen isn't going away. If anything, it's getting worse by the day. Here are a few questions every digital architect should ask themselves to ensure they aren't overwhelming their users by accident:

1. Have you thought about the limitations of attention when designing the layout of your Web site? If the magical number of the mind is less than four, then why do most sites fill our screen with dozens of options? Amazon, for instance, provides images of sixty different products on a twenty-seven-inch monitor. Indeed, one can fit a lot of information on a huge physical screen, but we have to remember the constraints of our much smaller mental screen.

2. Have you factored in the attentional environment? Our mental screen shrinks when we attend to multiple tasks. Here's one obvious suggestion: GPS screens in cars should adjust the amount of information displayed to our driving speed. When we are stopped at a red light, the screen can be fully functional, but if we're on the highway perhaps it should display nothing but the appropriate exit.

3. Have you looked for ways to compress information? My suggestion here is to consider using visuals instead of words whenever possible.

4. Have you considered ways to boost attention? As we will discuss in chapter 6, personalized videos grab a lot more attention than standard text formats.

5. Have you done a "whiteboard exercise"? Nobody sets out to create an overly complicated Web site that overwhelms users. Rather, such sites evolve that way over time, as new features, links, and multimedia effects are gradually added. Unfortunately, we often become blind to the drawbacks of these additions, as we fall for the "status quo bias." Thus, it's important to occasionally conduct a whiteboard exercise and design a new site that focuses only on the essential information. Notice that the best Web sites, such as Google, always try to strip away everything but the essential.

CHAPTER 2

———

Function Follows Form

FAST AESTHETICS

I'm going to conduct an experiment on you. It will require that you go to a Web site and look at a video clip. The clip itself consists of three different stimuli with brief pauses in between. During the pauses, I'd like you to rate the stimuli on a scale of 1 to 9 based on its visual appeal. You might not be able to make out what you see in the first exposure—in fact, it might be totally inexplicable—but I still want you to rate it. That's right, I'm asking you to have an opinion about a perception you can't explain. Sounds strange, I know, but please just play along. Here's the link: www.digitai.org/#lab. Once you are there, click on "Visual Appeal: Exercise Number 1."

All done? If you're like most people, the first clip was virtually impossible to perceive. That's because the image was flashed for fifty milliseconds, which is often too quick for conscious awareness. (To put that speed in perspective, the typical eye blink takes three to four hundred milliseconds.[1]) The second clip was a little longer—it flashed for five hundred milliseconds, or half a second. That's almost certainly long enough to perceive the picture, even if you can't quite comprehend it. Last, I showed you the static image for five seconds, giving you enough time to process many of its details.

Here's the strange part: If you're like most people, then your ratings for the Web site's visual appeal remained fairly constant across all three conditions. In other words, it didn't matter if I gave you fifty milliseconds or five thousand milliseconds—your opinion of what you saw remained the same.

It's worth taking a moment to appreciate just how bizarre this is. We typically assume that our aesthetic judgments are based on our conscious assessments, that we have to really see something before we can form an opinion about it. But what a series of experiments by Noam Tractinsky at Ben-Gurion University[2] and Gitte Lindgaard at Carleton University[3] demonstrates is that there's a very high correlation between ratings of visual appeal after extremely short exposures and ratings after much longer exposures. (To ensure that subjects weren't simply anchoring to their initial ratings, some of the studies randomized the order of each screenshot.) In short, we seem to render verdicts about the appeal of a Web site very, very quickly. What's more, these verdicts stay the same even when we're given far more time. We know what we like before we even know what we're looking at.

On the one hand, this is old news. Scientists have long known that people rely on unconscious processing and first impressions when perceiving the world. (There's a very fine line between unconscious and conscious influences, the precise timing of which depends on a long list of factors.)[4] In one widely cited study, subjects formed strong opinions about the character traits of strangers—such as whether they were trustworthy or aggressive—after viewing their faces for one hundred milliseconds.[5] Other research has repeatedly documented the power of subliminal priming, so that flashing subjects suggestive imagery—even when they don't consciously perceive it—can shift their beliefs and behaviors.[6] (One of my favorite examples is that showing people the Apple logo for a fraction of a second improves their performance on creative tasks.)[7] We like to think of ourselves as rational animals, fully aware of our preferences and their reasons. And yet, decades of psychological science clearly demonstrate that many of our choices, behaviors, and beliefs are rooted in processing that takes place *before* we even know what we're perceiving.[8]

Here's my hypothesis: I believe that screens might be exaggerating this human tendency. When it comes to our digital behavior, I think we are even more influenced than usual by these very fast verdicts generated by the unconscious brain. Because the online world is so visual, we easily slip into a more instinctive mode of thinking. It's not that screens are making us more superficial. Rather, the world of screens merely makes it easier for us to act on these superficial first impressions.

This is a speculative idea, to be sure. When I told John Payne, an eminent psychologist at Duke University (and a good friend), about my idea, his reply perfectly captured my attitude. "It feels right," he said. "But it would be nice to have at least one study showing that it's true."[9]

John is right—we don't have a study. *Yet.* Right now, we have barely half a study, the result of a pilot project John and I conducted with 360 subjects recruited at Universal Studios Hollywood. We were interested in how technology might affect the way people thought, especially when it came to complex topics requiring reflection. Subjects were randomly assigned to answer the questions on an iPhone, PC, or paper. Here's a sample question:

Imagine that the interest rate on your savings account was 1% per year and inflation was 2% per year. After 1 year, would you be able to buy:

A. more than today with the money in this account

B. exactly the same as today with the money in this account

C. less than today with the money in this account

The answer is C: when the rate of inflation exceeds the interest rate, keeping money in a savings account is a losing proposition, at least in terms of your purchasing power. Interestingly, subjects did significantly worse when answering this question on screens. While only 45 percent of people got it right on an iPhone, nearly 57 percent of people got it right when answering on paper. A similar pattern held for other financial questions, with paper subjects always outperforming their counterparts taking the quiz on iPhones or computers.

To repeat: this is a *very* preliminary result. Nevertheless, I think it fits with my hypothesis that people think faster on screens, and that this can lead us to become more reliant on our instinctive responses and initial impressions, even when they are misleading and incorrect.

But I don't think experiments are the only way to make the case. I think there is also a growing amount of indirect evidence that screens are changing the way we think, making us more impulsive and reactive. There is, for starters, the common complaint about the accelerating pace of the online world. We talk about how we feel chained to our e-mail inbox—we need to reply *right away*—and fret about our shortening attention spans, which leave us flitting from site to site, tweet to tweet. This lament is backed up by Web site analytics.

Tony Haile is the CEO of Chartbeat, a company that helps content providers understand the viewing habits of users. One of his most surprising findings is that most online clicks don't last for long. In fact, 55 percent of all visitors to a typical article spend less than *fifteen seconds* reading it.[10] This suggests that the average Web visitor isn't carefully assessing the content—they're just reacting to their first impression, making a quick decision to engage or look away. While this tendency might not matter for the assessment of pictures—additional looking probably won't change our initial judgment—it's probably not a great idea for text-heavy sites, because it takes time to process written information. We've traded away depth for speed.

And this doesn't just apply to stuff we read. Just look at Tinder, that very successful dating app. The mechanics of Tinder are simple: a user signs up by linking to their Facebook account. (This also serves as a means of verifying their identity.) Then, the app uses their geographic location and social network to suggest potential dates. When a new person is suggested, the screen is filled with a picture, followed by a brief biographical description.

Now comes the ingenious gesture that makes Tinder so popular: after a person is presented, the user can either swipe to the left (that means they're not interested) or swipe to the right (they are interested). If both people swipe to the right, the new couple is launched into a chat. Not surprisingly, the format of Tinder encourages quick assessments of other people, with the typical user able to assess dozens of strangers every minute. (Most speed-dating events, in contrast, require participants to spend three to eight minutes getting to know each other.) This helps explain why Tinder is currently processing more than 1.2 billion swipes every day.[11] It's a site designed to cater to our speedy first impressions. And since we basically make up our mind about other people in the first few hundred milliseconds anyway, why bother spending more time learning about their hobbies and favorite songs? Just swipe.

The pace of our thinking on screens, and the possibility that we might think even *faster* on mobile screens, is reflected in the prices shown to consumers. A recent study by researchers at Northeastern University found that many large retailers shift both their prices and mixture of products depending on whether a customer is shopping on their desktop computer or their smartphone.[12] Home Depot, for instance, served up a far more expensive selection of items to mobile users. While the average product generated by a Home Depot search on a desktop computer cost $120, the same search on a mobile device generated a list of results that cost, on average, $230. It's unclear why Home Depot engaged in this pricing strategy, but I wouldn't be surprised if it reflected the greater impulsivity of mobile consumers. After all, it's not very fun comparison shopping on your smartphone.

The sheer speed of our online decisions—whether it's choosing dates on Tinder or skimming articles on *The New York Times* or buying a lawnmower on HomeDepot.com—raises the obvious question. If first impressions strongly shape our online judgments, then what are these impressions based on? What variables influence our quick and sometimes subliminal opinions? The answer is obvious, if you think about it: they are based largely on aesthetics. If we are judging a Web site in fifty milliseconds, then we must be making a judgment about its appearance, just as our swipes on Tinder are based on the look of a stranger.

Computer scientists who study our online assessments refer to our swift judgments as rooted in a sense of "visceral beauty." That's a poetic way of saying that we react to how the look of something makes us feel. The visceral part refers to the fact that we often can't explain these feelings, since they are inspired by thoughts that take place outside of conscious awareness. The problem, of course, is that we can't ask people what they find "beautiful" or aesthetically pleasing, since they have no idea what they are responding to. The beauty remains an utter mystery.

Thankfully, there are ways of figuring out what people like to look at that don't involve asking them for an explanation. That's where we turn next.

MODELING BEAUTY

A few years ago, Katharina Reinecke, a computer scientist now at the University of Michigan, attempted to make sense of our online first impressions. She began by figuring out what people could actually notice in a fraction of a second. After reviewing the literature, she concluded that the most relevant aesthetic features—really the only things we could see right away—were "colorfulness" and "visual complexity." Before long, she began developing an algorithm that could automatically assess Web sites in terms of these two visual variables, and thus hopefully predict which sites people would prefer in advance of their actually looking at anything.[13]

Reinecke began with color. Numerous studies had already shown that colors could have a significant effect on our response to a Web site, reliably influencing our navigation and purchasing decisions. In one study by Naomi Mandel and Eric Johnson, subjects were shown a Web site that sold cars and asked to select which one they would buy.[14] Some students were shown the Web site with a red and orange background, while others were shown a green background complete with floating dollar signs. (The green condition was supposed to prime students to think about dollars and money.) As expected, those in the green condition were 31 percent more likely to choose the cheaper car, since the color and dollars made them more focused on price. While the vast majority of subjects didn't believe that the background color influenced their decision, Mandel and Johnson came to a very different conclusion.

Most Web sites, of course, are a bit more subtle than that; they don't use bright green background colors and pennies to trigger thoughts about money. Nevertheless, Reinecke wondered if the intensity and the range of colors might still influence our opinions of a Web site. To measure the intensity of color, Reinecke looked at the amount of nonwhite pixels on the screen; to measure the range of color, she analyzed the percentage of pixels that were close to the sixteen standardized colors that are part of the HTML 4.01 specification. (This allowed her to assess the familiarity of the shades on display; a lower percentage of pixels fitting the HTML specs meant that the Web site was using an unusual palette.) "When you start looking at colors [on Web sites], you see that there is quite a bit of variability," Reinecke says. "Some are very saturated, with black backgrounds and lots of contrast color. But others are mostly white with just a little bit of color."[15]

In addition to looking at colorfulness, Reinecke and colleagues also looked at "visual complexity," an aesthetic variable that measures the amount of information on a given site and how that information is presented. For instance, she hypothesized that more asymmetrical Web sites would feel more complex, as would those with more distinct groups of text, especially if they are not balanced over the space of the site. To quantify these factors, Reinecke relied on a "space-based" decomposition method, which automatically identified each text and image area. (A headline, in this model, counts as a separate "text group"; so does the subheadline and text body.) When the space-based analysis is complete, the site is reduced to a series of distinct "content regions," which allows the algorithm to figure out how symmetrical and dense it actually is.

Reinecke and colleagues then selected 450 different Web sites from a variety of genres, including 20 Web sites that had been nominated for Webby Awards. (Because she was interested in first impressions, Reinecke needed sites that subjects were seeing for the first time.) Each of the 242 volunteers was given a short online test, in which they were shown 30 different sites (randomly drawn from the larger set of 450) for five hundred milliseconds each. After viewing each Web site, the volunteers were asked to rate its visual appeal on a nine-point scale. Then they were shown the Web sites again, in a different random order, and asked to rate them for a second time. (Ninety-four percent of ratings were consistent across both trials, suggesting that visual appeal is a reliable variable.) The average ratings of the users were compared with the predicted ratings of visual appeal generated by the algorithm.

The results were impressive. According to the data, Reinecke's model explained 48 percent of the variation in aesthetic preferences for a given Web site. This means that nearly half of our immediate reaction to a given site—what we like and don't like—can be explained by looking only at colorfulness and complexity. "It was a cool finding," she says. "I think it shows us that a lot of the stuff maybe designers think is very important"—such as content and imagery—"isn't that important at all." In fact, this misplaced faith in irrelevant variables probably explains why those sites nominated for Webby Awards were no more appealing, on average, than a randomly selected site. Because these designers focused on the less relevant details of design, they ended up with underperforming sites.

To help you better understand how the model works, I'd like you to complete a short exercise. First, please watch the following short video clip, which can be seen here: www.digitai.org/#lab. (This time, click on "Visual Appeal, Exercise Number 2.") You will be shown five different Web sites for five hundred milliseconds each. I'd like you to rate each site on a nine-point scale of appeal.

Are you done? I showed you the sites in ascending order, so that the first one was the least appealing—it received just under a 2.0 out of 9 in Reinecke's tests—and the last one was the most appealing, getting an average rating of 7.0. I'm guessing that even though you barely had enough time to see the sites—and almost certainly couldn't read any of the words—you were fairly certain that the last designs were far better than the first ones.

So what were you responding to? Why do people think the last Web site was more than three times as appealing as the first one? According to Reinecke's research, the most significant variable, by far, is the visual complexity of a Web site. (Complexity was several times more influential than colorfulness.) In general, Reinecke found a strong negative relationship between high levels of complexity— these tended to be asymmetrical sites with lots of text and links— and ratings of visual appeal. But this didn't mean people wanted extremely simple sites, either: those also suffered in ratings of appeal, although not nearly as much as sites that were excessively intricate and dense. This means that the risk involved in calibrating a site's complexity is asymmetric: there's a small risk that the site will be too simple, and a big risk that it will be far too complicated. But the real aesthetic takeaway is that there's a tiny sweet spot of complexity, as those Web sites with a mean complexity rating around 4.2 on a nine-point scale were nearly twice as appealing as those with higher complexity scores.

And yet, even as Reinecke found a way to reverse-engineer our immediate aesthetic preferences, she wanted to understand the limitations of her model. She began by thinking about what it could *not* explain. This led her to focus on a stubborn fact of aesthetics, which is that not everyone finds the same stuff appealing. In fact, even in Reinecke's simple model of colorfulness and complexity, she noticed that demographic variables, such as age and education, were also correlated with visual appeal ratings. For instance, Reinecke found that levels of education were statistically related to preferred levels of colorfulness, as people with graduate degrees preferred Web sites with little color. (Interestingly, the same relationship held for those with only a high school diploma, who also disliked too much color.) Such differences suggested that people with different backgrounds and of different ages would prefer different kinds of Web sites. Beauty, as they say, was in the eye of the beholder.

To better understand these individual differences, Reinecke and Krzysztof Gajos of Harvard University collected 2.4 million ratings on the visual appeal of 430 different Web sites from nearly forty thousand participants.[16] (To get a diverse sample of subjects, Reinecke and Gajos created LabintheWild.org, a Web site that allows people from all over the world to participate in online experiments.) As before, they flashed a screenshot of a Web site for five hundred milliseconds and then asked subjects to rate its appeal on a nine-point scale.

The data confirmed Reinecke's suspicions: demographics strongly influenced our aesthetic preferences. In fact, they were so influential that even rudimentary demographic information could dramatically improve the performance of her aesthetic model. Let's begin with age: According to the data, subjects older than forty years of age showed a strong preference for more visually complicated Web sites. In some instances, the differences were stark, with older subjects rating complex sites as 60 percent more appealing than subjects under twenty years of age. In general, Reinecke found that the youngest subjects preferred sites that used saturated colors and larger images, while older subjects liked sites that were text-heavy and featured many distinct text groups, but used less saturated colors.

When it came to gender the main difference was colorfulness. For men, visual appeal peaked at a colorfulness level of 5.8. Women, meanwhile, gave the highest ratings to sites with a colorfulness level of 6.3. Men liked sites that used primary colors on a gray or white background, but women favored sites that used more homogenous color schemes and pastel shades.

Last, Reinecke and Gajos found that nationality exerted a strong influence on preferred Web site aesthetics. For instance, subjects from Mexico and Chile liked Web sites that were rated nearly twice as complex as subjects from Russia, while people in Malaysia favored sites that were far more colorful than people in Finland and Germany. (The United States is in the middle of the pack when it comes to levels of colorfulness and complexity.) What's more, these general cultural trends followed a predictable geographic pattern, so that "countries in close proximity share similar preferences"—Macedonia, Serbia, and Bosnia, for example, all preferred very colorful Web sites, while Finland and Russia preferred the lowest visual complexity. ("The results suggest that countries with a regular exchange of [cultural] values, e.g., due to migration, share similar website preferences," write the scientists.) Reinecke is currently trying to extend this work to include an analysis of rural versus urban preferences. Her initial data suggests that living in a big city increases our preference for more "modern website designs," featuring fewer colors and more streamlined layouts.

Toward the end of their paper, Reinecke and Gajos summarize the lesson of their research. For the first time, they say, designers will be able to maximize the appeal of their Web sites by relying on quantitative models of our first impressions. Instead of using trial and error, or obeying their aesthetic instincts, designers can use Reinecke's algorithm to predict, in advance, the appeal of their site. While it remains unclear why certain demographics prefer certain kinds of Web sites—Reinecke suspects that some of the age-related differences are driven by familiarity, as older subjects are more used to text-heavy documents—their impact is clear. Beauty on screens is no longer a black box: we can finally get some insight into what we like in a Web site, even if we can't explain these preferences.

I believe this research has major implications. Online first impressions are so important that it's only a matter of time before Web sites begin tailoring their look to reflect our actual unconscious preferences. The logical end point is an Internet in which the best Web sites and apps customize their appearance based on our demographic background. Are we an educated senior citizen from Poland? Then take away all the colors, and give us plenty of text and links. Are we a young Thai man? Then give us lots of bright color and imagery. (In Thailand, male subjects preferred bright pink and green color schemes.) "Some companies are already figuring this out a little," Reinecke says. She then notes that the McDonald's Chinese language site is full of information—reflecting the Chinese preference for higher levels of visual complexity—while the German site is very plain. Such aesthetic adjustments are currently done by hand, but it's easy to imagine a future in which each Internet user has his or her own "aesthetic algorithm," customizing the appearance of every site they see. Just as Pandora recommends music based on what I like, and Netflix sends me suggestions based on my viewing history, so might our browser automatically "format" Web sites in accordance with our visual preferences. Life is too short for ugly screens. And as we will soon learn, ugly screens come with a lot of negative side effects.

THE LOOK OF TRUST

A few years ago, the scientists Claudia Townsend at the University of Miami and Suzanne Shu at UCLA Anderson School of Management conducted a simple investigation into how aesthetics influence our investment decisions.[17] They randomly assigned 255 students to receive an annual corporate report. One of these reports was aesthetically pleasing—it had high-quality images and a clear layout. The other report was far less attractive: in a pretest, every single subject chose the pleasing report as having better "overall looks/ design." After perusing these two reports—both of which contained the exact same factual information—the subjects were asked to estimate the lowest acceptable selling price for shares of the company. In essence, they were asked to come up with a valuation of the company based on the information contained in the annual report.

If investors were rational agents, then the look of the report shouldn't have mattered—they should be responding only to its content. But that's not what happened. Townsend and Shu found that subjects in the "high aesthetic" condition—they were given the prettier document—insisted on an average selling price of $327.01 per share. Those in the low aesthetic condition, meanwhile, concluded that the company's shares were worth only $162.41. That's less than half as much! (In a subsequent study, Townsend and Shu found that aesthetics even influence experienced investors.) This research suggests that the design of the annual report can significantly influence our sense of value.

While Townsend and Shu looked at paper reports, the same logic applies to Web sites, as the visual appeal of a site has been shown to strongly influence all sorts of unrelated variables. A 2010 study by Swiss researchers, for instance, found that aesthetics dramatically affected a subject's perceptions of "usability," so that prettier cell phones seemed more functional, even when they were functionally equivalent to uglier versions.[18] (This might explain why Apple is so obsessed with the look of its operating systems and devices.) Although researchers once assumed that "usability" was the main factor driving our "involvement with a Web site"—people liked sites that were full of useful features—the latest studies suggest that our sense of usability is shaped, at least in part, by our instant aesthetic reactions. One of the credos of modernist design is that *form follows function*, that the look of a building or object should be shaped primarily by its intended purpose. But this research suggests that the credo is backward. When it comes to user assessments of design, *function follows form*.

And this pattern doesn't just apply to usability. In recent years, scientists have also looked at how aesthetics impacts our perceptions of trust. Do we find prettier Web sites more trustworthy? There's no logical reason why that would be the case, of course, but the human mind is full of illogical quirks. So far, the evidence suggests that the look of a site is highly correlated with our ratings of trust, a phenomenon often referred to as "the halo effect." In a 2011 paper led by Gitte Lindgaard, researchers showed that our first impressions of a Web site—they showed subjects screen shots for fifty milliseconds, which is too fast for conscious awareness—shaped our subsequent sense of trustworthiness. In short, if people found that the site was more visually appealing, they were far more likely to also think it was worthy of their trust.[19]

One of Reinecke's current experiments extends this line of inquiry. She showed people five-hundred-millisecond screenshots of dozens of different sites and then asked them to say how trustworthy the sites seemed. As expected, levels of trust were closely correlated with visual appeal. What was more interesting, perhaps, is that our trusting instincts bore almost no statistical relationship to the trustworthiness of the Web sites, at least as rated by the Web of Trust (WOT), a service that combines user reviews and independent measures to determine whether or not a site should be trusted. We probably shouldn't have more faith in better-looking Web sites, but we can't seem to help it.

In the digital world, the issue of trust is perhaps most relevant when it comes to our financial decisions. According to surveys, only 11 percent of Americans say they have a high level of trust in their financial institutions.[20] (More than 40 percent say they have "hardly any" trust.) While some of this distrust is certainly deserved—Lindsay Owens, a sociologist at Stanford, finds that distrust of banks spikes after major Wall Street scandals, such as the

Madoff affair[21]—it also comes with some very significant downsides. Consider the unbanked, those households that choose not to have a federally insured bank account. A recent FDIC report[22] concluded that one in thirteen households (or 8 percent of all Americans) were unbanked, with an additional 20 percent falling into the under-banked category. Because these households don't have a checking or savings account, or rarely use the accounts they do have, they are reliant on check cashiers and payday lenders that charge exorbi-tant fees and interest rates. (A typical payday loan, for instance, charges $15 for a fourteen-day $100 advance, which amounts to a *391 percent* annual interest rate.[23]) While there are many reasons people choose to forgo a bank account, one of the leading causes is a lack of trust in financial institutions.[24] They'd rather keep their cash in a shoe box.

Let's be clear: fixing the look of a Web site isn't going to solve this problem. But given the research on the halo effect, I also think improving the digital aesthetics might help. Right now, I fear that financial Web sites are making things worse.

Just look at the Bank of America landing page, which is currently the thirty-third most visited Web site in America according to Alexa .com, right after that of the *New York Times.*[25] With Reinecke's help, I ran my own detailed analysis of the Bank of America site.[26] The results suggest that the bank should rethink its Web strategy, or at least its online aesthetic. For instance, bankofamerica.com has an "average colorfulness" of 4.09, which is far outside the optimal level of 6.10. In fact, the banking Web site is too monochrome for almost every demographic group. (Only people in Finland, Poland, Russia, and a few other European countries would approve of the muted color scheme. They are, presumably, not the target audience.) The lack of colorfulness is particularly disagreeable to women, a customer group that the bank is actively pursuing.[27]

But this isn't Bank of America's only online problem: its Web site is also too complicated. According to Reinecke's algorithm, it scores 4.80 on the complexity scale, or half a point higher than the ideal of 4.23. This excessive complexity manifests itself in a number of ways. Here's one: the highest-rated site in Reinecke's survey contained fourteen links. Guess how many links are on the Bank of America home page? *Sixty-eight.* (And that's before you scroll down.) While the best sites tend to minimize their different text groupings, bankofamerica .com is cluttered up with words. In fact, the site contains fifteen different asymmetric text blocks, with the letters appearing in multiple fonts, sizes, and colors. Finally, Reinecke's research suggests the importance of clear menu bars, since they help users quickly navigate the site. Unfortunately, the Bank of America site is a case study in opaque navigation. At the top of the screen, there are three completely separate menu bars, in three different sizes. My concern is that these aesthetic issues might diminish our sense of trust, and thus lead to more underbanked and unbanked people.

It's easy to pick on Bank of America, but these are common errors. Reinecke's research demonstrates that the average Web site is, like bankofamerica.com, too colorless and too complicated. In her survey of several hundred sites, the average colorfulness was 5.17—the ideal was 6.10—while the average complexity was 4.80, which was significantly higher than the ideal of 4.23. Instead of using blocks of color to help users navigate the page, too many Web sites rely on words, words, and more words. Unfortunately, given the speed with which people process online information, all of this text ends up disorienting users. We don't have time to read. We barely have time to look.

If these Web site flaws were only a matter of aesthetics or appeal, it would be bad enough. But the data reveals that the unattractiveness of sites is directly related to other, more important issues, such as a perceived lack of usability and the absence of trust. These correlations might not be rational, but they still shape the perceptions of millions of consumers. Given these massive consequences, and the relative cheapness of a Web site redesign, it seems clear that we should revise our approach to online aesthetics. In the age of screens, there is nothing superficial about beauty.

OUR SUBLIMINAL FUTURE

Here's how I hope this research is used. I hope it makes Web sites take aesthetics more seriously. There's an old saying that you can't manage what you don't measure. By making it easier to measure aesthetics—Reinecke's algorithm can automatically scan a site and generate a score—I hope it persuades people that the look of a site is not a frivolous quality. Instead, it is tangled up with every other aspect of its performance, as prettier Web sites also feel more useful and trustworthy. Form has many functions.

But there are also some risks worth discussing. There is, after all, something deeply unsettling about the power of subliminal aesthetics. We are so used to thinking of our conscious selves as in charge that all the evidence documenting our lack of control—how much we depend on split-second perceptions and aesthetic judgments—is rather scary. What's more, screens might make us even more reliant on these unconscious preferences. We like what we like for reasons we can't begin to explain.

When it comes to taking advantage of these unconscious influences, the digital world opens up a raft of troubling new possibilities. Although the FCC has declared that subliminal advertising on television is "contrary to the public interest,"[28] and thus banned its use by any broadcaster using an FCC license, it has issued no such regulations for the Internet.[29] This is despite the fact that our online screens are an ideal venue for such subliminal messages. As the research consistently demonstrates, even a fifty-millisecond snapshot can strongly shape our subsequent behavior.

Furthermore, research by Linyun Yang and colleagues at Duke University has shown that, in some instances, making brands or products *harder* to see can actually increase our desire to buy the items. In a series of clever experiments, the scientists showed subjects a clip from BBC's *Planet Earth* interrupted by a television commercial for Mountain Dew. Some of the subjects were shown the commercial at regular speed; they had to watch all thirty seconds of the advertisement. In another condition, subjects watched the same clip but were shown the commercial at *ten times* regular speed, as if it were being fast-forwarded on a DVR. (It lasted for only three seconds.) In addition to manipulating the speed of replay, the scientists also altered the commercials paired with the Mountain Dew ad: half of the subjects were shown the ad in conjunction with a rugged Hummer ad—this fits the image of the soda—while the other half were shown a Honda ad. (Honda is considered dissimilar to the Mountain Dew brand.) Here's the unsettling result: those who watched the Mountain Dew ad in a blur were significantly more willing to buy the product, at least when it preceded a commercial for a dissimilar product, like a Honda minivan.[30]

What makes these results so disturbing is that they reveal how, in certain instances, making the stimuli *less* noticeable can actually increase their power. The problem, of course, is that we're then unable to explain what we're responding to, or why we're suddenly craving a can of Mountain Dew. We can't discount our desire for sweet soda by remembering the commercial, because we almost certainly don't remember watching it.

I can't help but worry about how such techniques might be used in the near future. I wouldn't be surprised if e-mail spam started taking advantage of unconscious priming, or if those ten-second video ads we have to sit through on YouTube began using subliminal stimuli. I'm not sure how effective such techniques would be, but I have no doubt someone will try them out.

My worries also extend to the business world. Let's say you run a company and you decide to invest in a beautiful Web site, tailored to the aesthetic preferences of your customers. Given the research, I'd say you made a wise investment. But perhaps you have an underhanded competitor. Maybe this competitor decides that it's cheaper to use subliminal messaging instead of creating a prettier site. And you know what? They might be right—*it is potentially cheaper*. It's also wrong. Nevertheless, you might find yourself losing customers to a competitor with an inferior product and site, simply because they are relying on a dubious psychological tactic, flashing us digital messages too fast for conscious awareness.

Another potential risk is that we'll learn to use these subliminal techniques on one another. Let me explain. I recently attended a pitch meeting for a new start-up that was looking for investors. Their product was simple: they were selling sexual emoticons. While most emoticons depict emotional states, such as smiling or frowning, these emoticons captured various sexual acts. I chose not to invest. :—)

But the pitch got me thinking. I realized that the allure of sex emoticons is that they allow people to send explicit texts without seeming *too* explicit. And this led me to wonder if such emoticons were only the first step on a slippery slope. In a few years, I could easily imagine a subliminal texting app becoming extremely popular. (Think Snapchat, but for the unconscious.) At first, the app will probably just seem like a party trick, allowing people to design thirty-to-fifty-millisecond images that appear in text messages to their friends. Maybe you want to flash them the message "Call me," or send them a subliminal photo from earlier in the day.

Sounds fun, right? But what happens if people start to get good at this? What happens if we figure out how to shift the behavior of the unconscious using subliminal images? Psychologists Keith Stanovich and Richard West famously divided the mind into two modes, "System 1" and "System 2."[31] The first system is fast and automatic, driven by emotions and instinct. It relies on cues we're often not aware of. System 2, on the other hand, is reflective and deliberate—it focuses on the information we're consciously paying attention to. My worry is that these subliminal images will tilt the balance of power toward System 1, making us even more reliant on its impulses. What's worse, we will have no idea what System 1 is so excited about, because subliminal stimuli are, by definition, invisible to System 2. So we'll be excited and motivated, without any ability to reflect on the causes of our amped-up emotional state. Given all the decisions we now make online, from buying groceries to picking dates, it's easy to see how such cues could come with big consequences. In fact, even if these subliminal pictures are only marginally effective, they could still have a massive societal effect by taking advantage of the scale of the digital world.

Obviously, this is a worst-case scenario. I don't know if it will happen. But I do hope regulators are also worrying about the possibility, and are thinking about how to update the rules on subliminal messaging for the twenty-first century.

The digital world is a world of our making, a visual environment we have created for ourselves. I don't think it's too much to ask that it be a safe and pretty place.

ASK YOURSELF

For too long, aesthetics has been dismissed as a superficial concern. That is a mistake. As the latest research demonstrates, the visual appeal of a Web site is tied up with far weightier issues, such as functionality and trustworthiness. Here are a few questions to help you get the most out of a Web site's design:

1. Have you "fast-tested" your site? Remember, you have only fifty milliseconds to impress your visitors. Flash your Web site to people for a very short period of time and then ask for their opinion. That is the opinion that matters.

2. Have you considered the implications of the halo effect? Perhaps the best way to increase the perceived usability and trustworthiness of your site is to make it prettier.

3. Have you taken the asymmetric nature of complexity into account? It's always better to err on the side of simplicity.

4. Who are your users? Remember that beauty is in the eye of the beholder, and that different demographics prefer different Web site styles. Is it time to personalize the look of your Web site and app?

CHAPTER 3

Display Biases

Have you ever played Battleship? It's a straightforward game. Each player positions his or her fleet of ships on a ten-by-ten grid. Then, the players try to guess where the other person's ships are hidden, picking a specific tile on the grid to target. The goal of the game is to sink the entire fleet. Winning is mostly a test of chance; the best strategy is to get lucky. The game has its roots in the First World War, as Allied naval fleets used their big guns with little guidance. The technology of artillery had leapfrogged the development of sonar, which meant that ships could fire at each other—they just didn't know where to aim.

I'd like to play a version of the game tilted in your favor. Instead of hiding only five ships on my board—that's the typical fleet size in the game—I'm going to hide *ten* ships. Your job is to hit them. I'll give you five guesses. Please mark your five shots on the grid below:

MARK YOUR FIVE SHOTS.

All done? Please turn the page to see where I hid my ships.

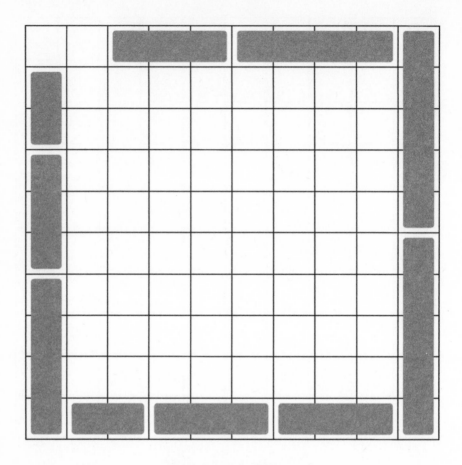

WHERE I HID MY SHIPS.

The mathematical odds suggest that you had an 88.1 percent chance of hitting at least one of my ships. But you probably didn't. And that's for a simple reason: human guesses in Battleship are not random. I can't read your mind, but I can make educated inferences about where you would look for my fleet. In fact, according to data compiled by Ruma Falk and colleagues, "seekers" in Battleship obey a predictable set of patterns.[1] In this chapter, we're going to learn what these patterns are, and why similar patterns play such a big role in shaping human behavior in the digital world.

In Battleship, the secret to winning is to avoid the hot spots of the grid when hiding your fleet, or those places where the eyes of your opponent are most likely to look. According to the scientists, the most commonly guessed spot on a five-by-five Battleship board—and it's guessed *three times* more frequently than random chance would suggest—is B4, which is the upper middle section of the grid. (In his experiments, Ayton used a five-by-five grid instead of a ten-by-ten grid, as in the official version of Battleship.) The next most frequently guessed spots are all clustered in the middle. In contrast, the edges of the grid are far less likely to be chosen. (They're guessed only half as frequently as you'd expect.) And that's why the outer rows are the best place to hide: by putting my ships there, I've reduced my chances of being hit by a factor of six, at least compared to a ship placed in the center of the grid.

This pattern of looking is known as the middle bias, and it's built into our visual system at a very fundamental level. As a result, it has big implications for any behavior closely linked to the act of looking. Consider radiologists, who spend most of their day staring at pictures from medical devices, such as CT scans and MRIs. Although radiologists go through years of specialized training, learning to carefully analyze every inch of the image, the evidence suggests they pay significantly more attention to the center of the screen, just like someone seeking ships on the Battleship board. In a clever 2013 study, Trafton Drew and colleagues at Harvard Medical School gave twenty-three trained radiologists a series of CT scans from real patients.[2] They were told to look for lung nodules, which can be an early indicator of lung cancer. What the radiologists didn't know is that a small picture of a gorilla had been slyly inserted into the top right corner of one of the CT scans. Although the gorilla was forty-five times larger than the typical nodule, 83 percent of the radiologists failed to notice it, and spent an average of only 250 milliseconds scanning that part of the image.

Or take military intelligence. If you're a CIA analyst staring at satellite pictures, or a drone operator looking at live streaming video, you are almost certainly less attentive to the edges of the display. (All of your attention is focused on the middle of the image.) The end result is that if there's relevant information along the border of the picture, then you are far less likely to detect it. The most important details will be hiding in plain sight.

Intelligence agencies typically deal with this problem by adding more eyes. Perhaps they split the original image into four smaller images, and then assign separate analysts to inspect each quadrant, searching for signs of terrorists or contraband or illicit activity. If that doesn't work, then they add even *more* eyes. In short, they assume they are dealing with a zoom problem, and that higher resolution and more eyeballs will lead to better detection.

But that's a dangerous assumption. The problem with subdividing the image, and then assigning each one to a separate analyst, is that more eyes also lead to more edges. (Each new picture comes with its own set of neglected borders.) The end result is an increase in the total number of blind spots. A much more effective solution, in my opinion, is to subdivide the relevant image into a series of overlapping ones, so that the borders of one picture are in the center of another. It's not about increasing the zoom. It's about eliminating the edges, making sure every part of the image is in the middle of somebody's vision.

While the middle bias is rooted in the habits of perception—it begins as a sensory quirk—it also influences our choices, as we are much more likely to select those options in the center of the visual field. This is true in Battleship, but it's also apparent in the retail environment. Nicholas Christenfeld, a psychologist at UC San Diego, has investigated how shoppers select products from the supermarket shelf. After watching real shoppers in a real market, he found that, when there were four rows of identical options, they selected one of the two middle rows 71 percent of the time. (That's 21 percentage points more than random chance would suggest.) Christenfeld found that a similar pattern even exists among toilet stalls. By keeping track of the number of times toilet paper needed to be refreshed in four stalls in a public restroom, he was able to show that the middle stalls were used roughly 50 percent more often than the outer ones. "These findings indicate that a substantial number of people do have implicit rules for deciding which option to choose when there is no objective basis for making a choice," Christenfeld wrote. "The data show not only that most people have such a rule, but also that the rule is widely shared."[3]

So what does the middle bias have to do with the digital world? While the bias itself isn't a new idea, there's suggestive evidence that it's becoming more important in the age of screens. (As usual, we need more research that directly compares the influence of these biases in offline and online settings.) The explanation for this is pretty straightforward: screens are a highly visual medium. Our phones, tablets, and computers cater to our sense of sight; those few inches of glowing pixels become a snapshot of the world, consuming all of our attention. (All of our other senses, from smell to hearing, are mostly neglected.) The end result is that technology is likely to increase the influence of our visual habits, at least when it comes to determining what we notice and choose. The middle has always been valuable real estate, which is why brands pay extra to be in the center of the supermarket shelf. But I believe that the digital world, because it is mostly visual, is making our visual hot spots even hotter.

I won at Battleship by figuring out where you wouldn't search for my fleet. The online world plays a similar game, except it's not about guessing where you won't look. It's about knowing where you will.

DISPLAY ENHANCED BIASES

The question of selective attention—what we notice on the screen—is the critical question of online psychology. As we saw in chapter 1, the surplus of information in the digital world has created a scarcity of attention, which means that getting people to look at the information you want them to see is an incredibly valuable skill. The future belongs to those who can engineer attention.

There are, of course, countless variables that go into human attention, from font size to the color palette of a Web site. (A lot of A/B testing is about fine-tuning these details.) However, one of the most powerful tools for influencing attention is also one of the simplest: screen location. We've just learned how location can influence the presence of blind spots, so that a detail in the wrong corner of the display will almost certainly be ignored, even if it's a picture of a man in a gorilla suit on a CT scan. But screen location turns out to be just as important during the decision-making process, as we use our eyes to assess our options. Look, for instance, at a recent paper led by Elena Reutskaja and colleagues.[4] The scientists used eye-tracking equipment to monitor the "first fixation" of a subject's gaze, or where they initially look on the screen. The experiment went like this: Forty-one Caltech undergraduates were asked, on a computer monitor, how much they liked various snack food items, such as Lay's potato chips and Snickers candy bars. After expressing their preferences, the subjects were then asked to make an actual choice. They were shown pictures of the same snack foods on a screen and told to pick the one they most wanted to eat at the end of the experiment.

While the subjects were scanning the screen, searching for their favorite junk food, the scientists were tracking their eyeballs, monitoring the spotlight of their gaze. Consistent patterns soon emerged, as people looked first and more often at items located in certain regions of the display. Where are these regions? The exact answer depended on the number of options shown on the screen. When only four snack foods were shown on a two-by-two matrix, people were most likely to look at the top left quadrant—their eyes settled there about half the time. (Of course, this result might flip for subjects who read languages, such as Hebrew or Arabic, in which the text is read from right to left.) However, as the choice set grew larger, a new trend began to emerge. When the subjects were shown nine options, their eyes first settled near the center approximately 99 percent of the time. When there were sixteen options, about 97 percent of their first fixations were on one of the four central tiles. What's more, these first fixations predicted their ensuing gaze, as the same spots that people looked at initially remained the most popular spots for subsequent fixations.

These patterns of eye fixations had a large influence on the choices of subjects, a phenomenon the scientists refer to as "display induced decision biases." Because the scientists had a record of their stated preferences—they knew which snacks people really wanted to eat—they could see how screen location influenced their eventual selections. Take the nine-option condition. When subjects were shown a screen filled with nine different snack foods, they were 60 percent more likely to choose the food in the center, regardless of what it was.

Think, for a moment, about what this means. Let's say a retailer really wanted to sell more of a particular item. By simply placing it in the screen locations that are most likely to exhibit first fixations, such as at the center of a screen, the retailer can dramatically increase its sales. In fact, when the scientists placed the worst snack in a popular screen location—say, the middle left—people were able to find the best option only about 30 percent of the time. However, when their preferred snack was in the center, they had a "choice efficiency" of 91 percent, which means they almost always made the best choice, selecting the food they most wanted to eat. That's a huge shift for what is ultimately just a simple design tweak. In the digital world, screen location is a hugely important variable.

The sheer magnitude of the screen location effect raises an interesting question about its origins. Why, exactly, are we drawn to whatever is in the center of the screen? Is it because the middle is inherently appealing? Or because the edges are not? Put another way, it's a debate about the relative importance of a "hot spot" in the center or a "cold spot" around the border.

The short answer is that we don't really know. Peter Ayton, for instance, speculates that these visual biases are rooted in an ancient fear of being on the edge of a crowd, since that leaves us more exposed to predators.[5] (The gazelle on the outside of a herd is more likely to get eaten by a lion.) As a result, Ayton suggests that the mind is wired to avoid edges of all kinds, whether it's the stalls in a bathroom or the snack food on the border of the screen. It's a clever theory, but as Ayton readily admits there's little evidence to support it.

Nevertheless, I think we get glimpses of an answer from existing research. Reutskaja and colleagues, for example, performed an indirect test of the middle bias by offering subjects either nine or sixteen options. If the screen location effect is mostly about an attraction to the middle, then we'd expect to see a large bump in people choosing the center when there are nine options as opposed to sixteen, since nine options presents people with a clear center alternative. Sure enough, there was a bump—it just wasn't that large. (The number of people fixating first on the middle region went from 97 percent when there were sixteen options to 99 percent when there were nine options.) These mixed results suggest that there are both cold spots and hot spots on the screen, that we are simultaneously drawn to the center and avoidant of the edges. That's why the middle bias exists even when there is no middle, and why it's even stronger when there is.

The larger lesson is that, in this new world of screens, the unconscious preferences of the visual system—where it looks, and how it looks—might play an even greater role in shaping our own preferences. While the screen location effect is a powerful example of this phenomenon, there are many other ways in which the mechanics of perception can influence what we choose. In a recent paper, a team of scientists led by Milica Milosavljevic at Caltech showed that even subtle changes to the visual prominence of an item can have a big impact on whether or not we choose it.[6] Their experiments, once again, involved offering undergraduates a selection of different snack foods. After being quizzed about their food preferences—they were asked to rank fifteen different snack foods from 1 to 15—the subjects had to choose between different combinations of food items on a screen. The visual prominence of the items was manipulated in two ways. First, the scientists selectively increased or decreased the brightness of one of the items, so that a bag of M&M's might be lit up while every other item was dimmed. The second thing they did was alter the exposure time of the food choices, displaying them for various durations between seventy milliseconds and five hundred milliseconds.

These manipulations of saliency—the ease with which subjects could see their options—had a large impact on their snack selections, especially when the subjects didn't have extremely strong brand preferences to begin with. (If you really don't like peanuts, then making the Snickers logo much brighter won't trick you into picking it.) Perhaps the most remarkable finding is that changes in visual saliency can get people to choose snacks that violate their stated preferences about half of the time. In other words, if you prefer Doritos to Lay's, then there's a good chance that making the Lay's bag a little easier to see on a screen will get you to reverse your preferences. The effect was even more powerful when subjects had to choose a food while simultaneously performing a simple arithmetic task, a condition of "cognitive load" designed to simulate the distractions of the multitasking life. This suggests that the typical way we behave online—say, shopping on J.Crew while scanning our Facebook feed and responding to texts on our phone—magnifies the biases of the visual system.

This is an unsettling result. We like to imagine our choices as reflections of our conscious desires. We want to believe that we will always pick the snack food we most want to eat. But this data suggests that our choices are often shaped by the perceptual habits of the eye, which are drawn to certain items and areas of the screen. Sometimes, salience matters more than preference.

Why does salience matter so much on screens? One likely answer has to do with the speed of the digital world. According to the eye-tracking data, first fixations occur around 350 milliseconds after people are exposed to the different foods on the screen. (To put this number in perspective, it takes the typical person about that long to become consciously aware of a bodily movement.)[7] This means that the visual system is shaping our decisions long before we've even had a chance to consider our options; the mechanics of sight precede the deliberations of the mind. As we saw in chapter 2, such processing speed is a hallmark of the online world, as our choices on screens are occurring at an ever quicker pace. When people are given more time, when they're allowed to leisurely contemplate their junk food options, these visual biases become less important.[8] But screens rarely inspire such deliberate thinking. Instead, they often lead people in the opposite direction, so that we keep making more and more decisions in less and less time. The end result is that the first fixations of the eyes are increasingly making our choices for us.

THE CHOREOGRAPHY OF VISUAL ATTENTION

As your eyes move across this page, reading this word and then the next one, they engage in a predictable set of movements. Although the reading process feels smooth and continuous, that feeling is an illusion. In reality, your eyes flit across the page, leaping from letter to letter and skipping many in between. These movements are known as saccades and they are controlled by a set of small muscles grafted on to the eyeball. Although we have conscious control over our gaze—we can choose where to look, and when to look away—saccades are almost entirely unconscious. You might know what you're reading. But you have no idea how you're reading it.

Consider the following sentence. I'd like you to count every occurrence of the letter *f*:

FINISHED FILES ARE THE RESULT OF YEARS OF SCIENTIFIC STUDY COMBINED WITH THE EXPERIENCE OF YEARS.[9]

How many *f*'s did you find? The most popular answer is three. The correct answer is six. (If you got the answer wrong, it's probably because you missed the *f*'s in "of.") Since experienced readers tend to skip over function words such as *and*, *if*, *the*, and *of*—one study estimated that our eyes skip over 65 percent of them[10]—it's not too surprising that you couldn't find the *f*'s even when you were looking for them.

The nonrandom nature of eye movements has big implications for the layout of information on screens, because it turns out that your eyeballs don't spend equal amounts of time on every pixel. Rather, they move in a series of flights and perches, which can be predicted in advance. While first fixations reveal the parts of the screen that attract our eyes, their path *after* that fixation is also not random. Instead, it is subject to a short list of tendencies and rules, which shape the ways in which we forage for information.

Look, for instance, at a seemingly minor design decision: whether to list the options in columns (vertical format) or rows (horizontal format). I've talked to numerous Fortune 100 firms about this variable on their Web sites. I always begin with the same question: Why did they do it this way? The answer has been consistent—they don't know. That's just how the site came out. They gave the choice of columns and rows little consideration because they assumed it didn't really matter, that the layout wouldn't influence the choices of their customers.

That's probably a mistaken assumption. In a classic 1977 paper, the psychologists James Bettman and Pradeep Kakkar asked 150 housewives to choose one of eleven breakfast cereals, each of which was rated on thirteen different attributes, such as price, size, etc.[11] For some women, the options were organized by brand: they first selected a label (say, Kellogg's) and then looked at its qualities. The other women were asked to choose among cereals organized by attribute, so that they looked first at the different features and only then at the brands. This change in the layout—arranging alternatives either by brand or by attribute—dramatically altered the ways in which the women assessed their options. When the information was organized by attribute, the women searched along those lines; the opposite occurred when the cereals were organized by brand. Although traditional theories of consumer choice focus on making information *available* to consumers, Bettman and Kakkar pointed out that the format of the information is just as important. "The strategies used to acquire information are *strongly* affected by the structure of the information presented," they wrote. "In effect, consumers process information . . . in the form it is given."

The importance of these design considerations has likely grown in the age of screens. Look, for instance, at a new eye-tracking study led by Savannah Wei Shi at Santa Clara University and published in *Management Science*. While the study confirms previous results on the importance of layout, it also reveals a set of visual biases rooted in the movements of the eyes across the screen.[12]

Perhaps the most important of these visual movement biases involves a strong built-in preference for moving from side to side, in a sweeping horizontal motion. (The scientists speculate that this bias is rooted in the sensory properties of the retina.) As a result, information that appears in a horizontal context tends to have higher saliency—we're more likely to notice it.

To explore these ideas in a real-world setting, Shi and colleagues had subjects choose a desktop computer on the Dell Web site (www .Dell.com). For years, the Dell Web site has listed the different computer models as columns, with the attributes of each model arranged in horizontal rows. (For a typical desktop, there might be twelve different attributes, including price, processor, monitor, operating system, and warranty.) During the experiment, some subjects were randomly assigned to pick a computer using the current layout of the Dell Web site, while others looked at a transposed version, in which the products (and not their attributes) were presented in horizontal rows. As expected, these different formats led to very different styles of information processing. When the products were in horizontal rows, the typical user focused less on the attributes and spent more time (relatively speaking) looking at the products. In contrast, putting attributes in horizontal rows led subjects to compare a single attribute, such as price or processing power, across various models. Interestingly, the choices of the subjects were tightly correlated with the cascades of their gaze, as attributes and products that received more visual attention proved more influential. This suggests that if a subject spent a lot of time looking at the price variable, then they might become more price sensitive. The opposite might happen if their visual system settled on a more expensive product. It's as if the eyes choose first.

When designing the layout of information, these movement biases can be used to help people pay attention to the most necessary facts.

By putting more important details in the most likely path of the eyes—away from the edges and in the horizontal plane—we can increase the likelihood that these details will get noticed. Just as stores attract more customers when they're located on streets with higher foot traffic, so does information attract more attention when arranged to maximize eye traffic.

We're only beginning to understand how the biases of the eyes shape the thoughts of the mind. Nevertheless, it's already clear that the highly nonrandom habits of the visual system must be carefully considered, for the uniformity of the display is an illusion; every inch of digital real estate is not of equal value. We aren't aware of these perceptual rituals, but they still determine what we perceive and choose. In a world of screens, the act of looking has never mattered more.

ASK YOURSELF

The digital age has likely amplified the importance of our visual biases. Unless you are taking these perceptual habits into account, you are missing a powerful opportunity to increase the impact of your information. After all, it's possible to make people look, but it's much better to be where they're already looking.

To help you maximize the opportunity (that is, being in the hot spots) and minimize the risk (that is, being in the cold spots), I have compiled the following list of guiding questions.

1. Have you considered the middle bias? Just as items in the center are more likely to be chosen on a supermarket shelf, so does the placement of items on the screen dramatically affect our choices. For example, many people will select a snack they don't care for, merely because it is in the middle of the screen.

2. Have you considered the top-left bias? In situations where a middle choice doesn't exist—say, a screen divided into a two-by-two matrix—our eyes gravitate toward the top-left cell.

3. Have you considered potential cultural differences in display biases? My native language is Hebrew, which is read from right to left. I speculate that those used to reading right to left might gravitate toward the top-right cell.

4. Have you considered "cold spots"? There are hot spots on the screen, but there are also cold spots. In the Battleship game, for example, you want to hide your ships in the cold spots (which are the edges of the screen), because they are six times less likely to be selected than the middle of the screen. Of course, if you're an online retailer, then you don't want your high-margin items to be placed in the cold spots, as that will make them much less likely to be chosen.

5. Have you considered the possibility that visual biases might be enhanced on screens? In one study, the vast majority of radiologists missed a gorilla on CT scans they reviewed on screens. I suspect they might not have missed it so frequently on an old-fashioned film, but we obviously need a lot more research to test my hunch.

6. Have you considered the blind spots generated by zooming in? If you are an intelligence analyst searching for terrorists, you might be tempted to zoom in, but that means that a lot of the battlefield is being pushed to the edges, which are often our blind spots. You must think carefully about how you take that snapshot of the "battlefield," if only to ensure that you are not missing critical intelligence.

7. Have you considered the horizontal bias? Our retina is programmed to search the world horizontally. As a result, any information displayed in rows receives greater decision weight than information displayed in columns.

8. Have you factored in decision speed? The faster we search and choose, and the more we attempt to multitask, the stronger our visual biases are.

CHAPTER 4

——

The New Mirror

YOU CAN'T HIDE

A few years ago, I bought a Nike FuelBand, one of those rubber gadgets that keeps track of your physical activity. I was looking for a watch—I had my eye on a nice Swiss timepiece—but I thought the FuelBand looked even cooler, with its matte black bracelet and tiny LED lights. Plus, the device might help me get in better shape. Even a Rolex can't do that.

For the most part, the FuelBand has been a disappointment. While I still think it looks nice, I rarely use it to do anything except tell time. It hasn't helped me lose weight or take more steps during the day; I've learned to tune out its annoying reminders. At this point, it's little more than a piece of jewelry with batteries.

In part, the FuelBand is limited by its technology, as its measurements of my physical exertion are imprecise. Because the gadget monitors only arm movements, any exercise that doesn't involve swinging limbs, such as pushing a stroller or yoga, barely registers at all. (Brushing your teeth gives you more "fuel" points than push-ups.) What's worse, the short battery life is a constant headache. It's not uncommon for the power to run out over the course of a day—and for me not to even notice.

These are fixable problems, of course: our digital gadgets keep getting better. The first-generation Apple Watch represents a huge improvement over my old FuelBand, and I'm sure the next-generation Apple Watch will be even more refined. (For one thing, the Apple Watch uses GPS to record activities, such as cycling, that can't be measured in steps.) One day, we might even get a wearable computer that doesn't need to be charged every single day.

But the biggest problem with these gadgets isn't technological, at least not in the traditional sense of the word; it doesn't involve lithium ions or crude motion sensors. Rather, I believe that these devices are most limited by the ways in which they give us feedback. In many cases, the wearables assume that feedback alone is enough, and that merely providing people with relevant information will solve the problem. But that's not the case. The ordinary bathroom scale, for instance, offers us all the feedback we need about our weight. It's cheap, reliable, and doesn't suffer from any battery issues. And yet, it has most definitely not solved the obesity crisis.

That's because the existence of feedback is only the first step. If the FuelBand and Apple Watch are going to fulfill their stated purpose—helping me live a healthier life—then they have to convey all that feedback in a form that convinces me to get up from my desk and increase my heart rate. In this sense, the real challenge of these wearables involves the ways in which the technology interacts with the user, and how their constant stream of information is designed and displayed. If this interaction isn't properly managed, then the gadgets will always just be fashion accessories with microchips, taking up valuable space on my wrist.

Of course, these wearable watches are merely a small example of a far larger trend: we are becoming more and more reliant on screens and machines for feedback about our lives. For the first time in human history, we can monitor our body and behavior in exquisite detail, keeping track of everything from the amount of sleep we get to the number of calories we swallow. We can track our steps and resting pulse, our social network and spending habits. (There's even a smartphone app that can tell you how often you check your smartphone.) Thanks to the plunging price of mechanical sensors, it's now possible to automatically quantify aspects of life that, only a few years before, would have required a trained team of professionals. Technology has become an omnipresent mirror.

This new world of feedback even extends to other people. There are reviews of sellers on eBay and renters on Airbnb; Uber passengers review their drivers (and vice versa), while students review their professors. We can even review our exes. Lulu, a dating app that launched in early 2013, arrived with a simple premise: it allowed women to anonymously comment on men they'd dated. (It was initially marketed as "Yelp for men" and promised it would "unleash the value of girl talk.") Women are encouraged to describe the charms and foibles of the men they know; some popular hashtags on the site are #Leavesaftersex or #Majormommyissues. In short, Lulu extends the feedback trend to the realm of personal relationships, allowing every future date to know about a man's past behavior.

This chapter is about the impact of all this new digital information, how these new mirrors are changing the way we think about ourselves and the world around us. While it'd be nice if feedback by itself were sufficient, that clearly isn't the case. Rather, the latest research demonstrates that digital feedback is useful only if done right, in accordance with a set of behavioral principles. This chapter is about those principles. It's about how we should give people feedback on screens that results in changing behavior, whether it's losing weight or cutting spending or getting more exercise. It's about how to make these new mirrors *better*.

THE UPSIDE

Several years ago, the psychologists Avraham Kluger and Angelo DeNisi conducted an authoritative review of feedback interventions on human performance. They looked at 607 different experiments and 23,633 distinct experimental observations. They analyzed feedback trials for fighter pilots and kids learning how to read, for factory workers on an assembly line, and for dieters trying to lose weight. Such a study is known as a meta-analysis, as the scientists were trying to discern general trends from a very large and varied body of research.[1]

What did Kluger and DeNisi find? While feedback interventions improved performance on average, in about 38 percent of cases the feedback actually led people to do *worse*. The dieters gained weight; the students struggled to learn; the workers were less productive. It's a sobering finding, a reminder of just how hard it is to structure effective feedback.

As we'll soon see, the same pattern extends to the digital world: some feedback on screens makes us perform better and other feedback makes us perform worse. And while there are many variables that influence the impact of digital feedback, I think the single most important variable has to do with quantity. Not surprisingly, too little feedback stifles learning—we don't improve because we don't know how we're doing, let alone how to do better. But too much feedback, which is a big risk for the online world, can be just as problematic. Sometimes, this feedback overload just makes us tune out; we end up ignoring all the information, even when it might be helpful. But the overload can also lead us to overreact, which makes a bad situation even worse. Instead of inspiring better decisions, it ends up doing the opposite.

The technical term for this phenomenon is an inverted U-curve, which is a fancy way of saying that one can have too much of a good thing. As the quantity of feedback increases on the x-axis, the positive returns from that feedback rapidly decrease. The benefit has become a cost.

Let's start with the good news, those forms of digital feedback that improve our behavior. For the most part, this feedback works because it uses the reach of the digital world to provide us with needed feedback that didn't previously exist. One way to think about it is in terms of that upside-down U-curve. If before we were on the far left side of the curve—suffering from the absence of feedback—we are now in the sweet spot, able to use this new information to improve our decisions.

Consider a form of feedback that is unique to the digital world: real-time financial information. Until recently, the only way to get up-to-date details about your bank account was to call your bank or visit a branch. The same was true of credit cards and investment accounts—most people didn't know how much money they'd saved or spent until the monthly statement arrived in the mail.

But the rise of smartphones and mobile computing has changed all that. Every big bank now has an app, allowing customers to monitor their balances from anywhere; the same is true of major credit cards. To understand the potential implications of these new forms of feedback, Yaron Levi, a Ph.D. student at UCLA, and I decided to study users of a Web site called Personal Capital, a much-praised service that allows an individual to link all of his or her financial accounts in a single place.[2] The star attraction of Personal Capital is the dashboard, in which users can track their investment performance and spending behavior at a glance. For instance, the dashboard breaks down, by category, where the money goes; it shows you how much you spend at clothing stores and on entertainment, how much goes to transportation, and the percentage of income that's devoted to paying off the mortgage. What's more, this feedback can be accessed at any time, from nearly anywhere. Yaron and I were interested in how all this new financial information would impact the purchasing decisions of consumers.

We focused on a subset of longtime Personal Capital users who downloaded the mobile app shortly after its release. Because these subjects had previously been visiting the Web site, we were able to focus on the impact of the app on their spending habits. The first thing we discovered is that app users got far more feedback. While Personal Capital Web users viewed their financial dashboard an average of 2.14 times per month before installing the app, that number jumped to 12.47 times per month after installation. It's important to note that this increase was entirely driven by new mobile views, as Web site visits stayed constant; the app was additive, and not a substitute.

Here's the punch line: all of this new financial feedback significantly influenced people's spending decisions, with the typical app user decreasing their monthly spending by 15.7 percent. Not surprisingly, almost all of this decrease came in the form of discretionary spending, with users spending far less on items such as dining out. These results fit with recent government surveys, which find that most consumers with access to their financial information on mobile phones check their balances before making large purchases. Of those who check, 50 percent decide *not* to buy an item because of the feedback.[3] It only makes sense, then, that making this information far easier to access, and giving consumers information about all of their accounts in one place, would lead to even more responsible spending habits.

To put this field result in perspective, it's worth considering other attempts to help consumers spend less money and save more. In a study, a team of economists led by James Choi at Harvard University looked at the saving behavior of Americans.[4] While 68 percent of respondents reported that their savings rate was too low, only 3 percent of respondents actually increased their contribution rate to their 401(k). In a separate study, subjects attended a one-hour seminar on retirement savings. Among those subjects who were not yet enrolled in a 401(k), all the attendees said they wanted to start saving. Sadly, only 14 percent ended up enrolling after the seminar. If these new 401(k) enrollees saved at the typical rate of 6 percent, then the expensive and time-consuming seminar would have increased the average savings rate for the total pool of attendees by less than 1 percent (14 percent times 6 percent). They should have given them an app instead.

There are, of course, numerous caveats to our finding in the Personal Capital study that the right information at the right time can dramatically cut spending. For starters, the impact might not last—we have data only from the four months following app installation.

It's possible users might stop checking their accounts and revert to their old spending habits. Second, Personal Capital users tend to be younger, wealthier, and more tech-savvy than the general population. More research is needed to ensure that these results hold true for everyone else, too.

Nevertheless, I think our data is a clear example of just how big an impact digital feedback can have, at least if it falls on the right spot of the inverted U-curve. Although the Personal Capital app itself provides little guidance—it doesn't tell you not to spend money, or how much to save—consumers were able to extrapolate from the information. They knew what they needed to do, provided they got feedback when they needed it most, which is when they were making a purchasing decision. Sometimes, timing is everything.

There is a larger lesson here. Excess consumer spending is often described as a problem of limited self-control—consumers don't have the willpower to forgo a purchase. And given the intransigence of many self-control problems—the American obesity rate, for instance, has slowly gotten worse despite a long list of interventions—it's easy to lose hope, to assume that we can't do anything to boost our discipline. However, our field study is a reminder that we can change, and that a simple app offering straightforward feedback can dramatically enhance our ability to exert self-control.

Here's another example of the far-reaching positive effects made possible by feedback. It comes from Philip Tetlock, a psychologist at the University of Pennsylvania. Tetlock is probably best known for his work on expert predictions.[5] A few decades ago, he began following more than 280 people who made their living "commenting or offering advice on political and economic trends." His roster included political scientists, economists, journalists, and even intelligence analysts.

Every few months, Tetlock would ask these experts to make predictions about various future events. Would inflation rise? Who would win the next presidential election? Would Quebec secede from Canada? By the end of the study, Tetlock had quantified the responses to roughly 27,500 different forecasting questions.

After Tetlock tallied up the data, it became clear that the vast majority of experts were not very helpful; their guesses barely beat random chance.[6] There is no simple explanation for these failures of prediction. The inaccuracies of the experts were driven by a long list of cognitive biases, from overconfidence to a tendency to envision only a single possible future. Instead of taking contradictory evidence into account, many pundits preferred, Tetlock says in an essay cowritten with Dan Gardner, "keeping their analysis simple and elegant by minimizing 'distractions.'"[7] What's worse, they rarely took their past performance into account or learned from their predictive failures. Unfortunately, this meant that they never learned how to do better—their predictive accuracy was stuck at a pitiful level.

But don't despair: Tetlock's latest work demonstrates that it's possible to dramatically improve our predictive performance, provided we get the right amount of feedback. We won't become omniscient, but at least we'll know what we do and do not know. In a long-term study funded by the Intelligence Advanced Research Projects Activity (IARPA), a division of the American intelligence community, Tetlock and colleagues tried to see if they could use feedback to enhance the predictions of a few thousand amateur volunteers. (The only "requirement" is that volunteers have a bachelor's degree, although even that requirement can be waived.[8]) After identifying some of the most promising individual forecasters—these volunteers seemed less prone to the biases that afflict so many pundits—Tetlock asked them to make predictions about various current events, from the likelihood of arms inspections in Syria to the future of Venezuelan gas subsidies. The volunteers were then given extensive feedback about their predictions—they learned when they were right and, more important, when they were wrong—and taught how to avoid the most common cognitive errors. After three years, this simple system generated several striking results. In particular, it has led to the emergence of what Tetlock calls "superforecasters," people who are able to consistently beat other experts and algorithms. In many instances, the victories were resounding, with the superforecasters proving to be 35 to 65 percent more accurate than their competitors. They even beat intelligence analysts at the CIA with access to classified information.[9]

Tetlock's research demonstrates, in a real-world setting, that effective feedback is a key element of effective thinking. When it comes to prediction, one of the most efficient ways to improve is to create an "outcome relevant learning structure," in which people receive constant updates about the accuracy of their forecasts. (In other words, they keep score.) In fact, Tetlock notes that one of the reasons superforcasters were possible in the IARPA tournament (and not in his original survey of experts) is that their forecasts were about events closer in time, thus enabling them to receive more timely feedback. The digital world, of course, makes such feedback structures far more manageable. Not only is it easier to keep track of predictions, but we can deliver the feedback in a more timely fashion, thus maximizing its learning potential. (In the analog world, it's hard work keeping track of predictions, thus making it easy for experts to ignore their incorrect ones.) Tetlock, for instance, has imagined building on the IARPA program to create an online system that can automatically record and track human forecasts. "Imagine running tallies of forecasters' accuracy rates," he wrote with Dan Gardner. "Imagine advocates on either side of a policy debate specifying in advance precisely what outcomes their desired approach is expected to produce . . . and the conditions under which participants would agree to say 'I was wrong.'"[10] According to Tetlock, such a feedback mechanism would have huge benefits, improving the signal-to-noise ratio of public discourse and sharpening academic debate. "At a minimum," he writes, "it would highlight how often our forecasts and expectations fail." In a world of overconfident experts, a new mirror just might be the best way to stay humble.

THE DOWNSIDE

It would be nice if more feedback were always better, if the world could be cured of its ills by a legion of smart sensors telling us all about ourselves. Alas, that's definitely not the case; mirrors can't solve everything. In fact, getting too much feedback—pushing people to the far right side of the inverted U-curve—is sometimes worse than none at all. That's because providing people with new digital information is merely the first step—what's much more important is figuring out how users will respond to it.

Take, for instance, feedback about investing decisions. While Personal Capital's mobile app helps consumers cut their spending, the same can't be said about feedback related to our investment portfolio. In my research with Richard Thaler, we found that a greater amount of feedback in this domain can trigger a mental error known as myopic loss aversion.[11] That's a technical term for a very common mistake, which occurs when investors make decisions based on short-term losses in their portfolio, even when they should have a long-term investment plan.

Consider what happens when you check the daily returns from the S&P 500 stock market index.[12] If you check every single day, then there's a roughly 47 percent chance that the market will have gone down. But what happens if you check the S&P once a month? The numbers will then start to look a little better, as the market will have gone down only 41 percent of the time. Years are better still, as the S&P generates a positive return seven years out of every ten. And if you check once a decade—we calculated this using overlapping decades—then you're going to get bad news about the market only about 15 percent of the time.

Why does this matter? There's solid evidence that experiencing such losses—noticing that our portfolio is losing money—leads to poor choices. In one lab experiment by Richard Thaler, Amos Tversky, Daniel Kahneman, and Alan Schwartz, subjects were far more likely to invest in a bond fund when feedback was given more frequently. Unfortunately, these low-risk bonds also generate lower returns over the long haul. As the scientists noted, "Providing such investors with frequent feedback about their outcomes is likely to encourage their worst tendencies. . . . More is not always better. The subjects with the most data did the worst in terms of money earned."[13] Such is the vicious circle of loss aversion, as our strong dislike of losses causes us to lose even more.

And this brings us back to the digital world. Given the profusion of connected devices, I think most people will end up looking at their investment portfolio far more frequently. (It's not easy to delete the Apple stock app, which comes preinstalled on the iPhone and Apple

Watch.) Over time, this abundance of feedback will make us more vulnerable to myopic loss aversion, since the more often you check the S&P 500, the more likely it is to have gone down. As a result, the time horizon of our investment behavior will shrink to reflect the frequency of feedback. This is obviously a terrible idea. If your 401(k) has a thirty-year time horizon—that is, you aren't planning to retire for another few decades—then you shouldn't obsessively monitor your short-term losses, as that will lead to investment behavior that is too conservative. In a paper done with Richard Thaler, for instance, we found that the average investor behaved as if he or she had a one-year time horizon—as if they would liquidate within a year—which led them to underinvest in the stock market and over-invest in bonds.[14]

But that finding is twenty years old. We conducted our study long before Goldman Sachs had an iPhone app or people could buy and sell investments with a few swipes of the thumb. My current concern is that, thanks to the high frequency of investing feedback— we are now on the extreme right side of the U-curve—people will develop even shorter time horizons, which could lead to even worse performance. This suggests that myopic loss aversion is a behavioral principle that's likely amplified by the online world, with adverse outcomes for the typical investor. To be sure, I'm not making predictions about the future of the stock market: I have no idea what's going to happen. But I do wonder if we might soon reach a point in which high-feedback investors are not even willing to hold *bonds*, since bonds sometimes go down. They might insist on cash instead.

This new digital information could also harm our investing decisions by making us more sensitive to market bubbles. Consider a recent experiment led by Benedetto De Martino.[15] In the experiment,

Caltech students were asked if they wanted to invest in a bubble market, a situation in which the price of an asset was much higher than its fundamental value. (The value of the stock was based on its future payments of a dividend.) Here's where things get interesting: subjects who were more attuned to the behavior of other investors—and De Martino and colleagues measured this using a standard behavioral task and brain imaging—were also more likely to invest in the speculative bubble. "Normally, in everyday social encounters and in specialized professions, this kind of mind reading is useful to the individual," said Colin Camerer, one of the authors of the paper, in an interview published in 2013.[16] "But in these markets, when prices are going crazy, these people think, 'Wow, I think I can figure these markets out. Let me buy and sell.' And that is usually going to contribute to the bubble's momentum and also cost them money." While economic theory has long assumed that bubbles are caused by so-called dumb money—these are investors who are lacking relevant information about the speculative investments—this new research suggests that bubbles might also be accelerated by an excess of feedback. Similar results were found in an experiment by Terry Lohrenz, Meghana Bhatt, and colleagues at Virginia Tech.[17] By having subjects play an investment game together, the scientists were able to show that people in the market naturally imitate one another, even when it leads them right off a cliff. (The scientists used actual historical bubbles, such as the Nikkei in 1986, in their study.) Our irrational exuberance is contagious, and it can spread extremely fast on screens.

A similar problem exists after the market bubble is popped. Just imagine what will happen during the next serious market correction, as tens of millions of investors watch their life savings evaporate in real time on their smartphones and tablets. At such moments, it's awfully hard to stay calm, let alone think about long-term returns. And that's why the average investor would probably benefit from *less* feedback during a crash, which would make it easier to avoid the sort of impulsive sell-offs and herding behavior they will later regret.

What's more, digital devices make it even easier to act on these errant instincts driven by too much feedback. Two decades ago, we almost certainly had to call our broker with a buy or sell order; if it was a really bad decision, made in the midst of a bubble, he or she might have been able to talk us out of it. But now we can make major trades with a few taps on our phone. It's so easy to make financial decisions that we might not give the decision enough thought.

Both of these investment examples are a reminder that feedback exists in a human context. While the extra financial information might be well intentioned—shouldn't we make it easy for people to check their portfolio?—the subsequent reaction of investors must be taken into account. Take the results of a real-world experiment studied by Maya Shaton.[18] On January 1, 2010, Israeli government regulators made a seemingly minor change involving the kind of information investors were given about their retirement accounts. Before the rule change, the returns of most accounts were displayed on a monthly basis—investors were told how their investments had done during the prior thirty days. The new regulation, however, prohibited highlighting returns for any period shorter than a year. While investors could still access the short-term returns if they wanted, it took a little bit of effort. Most people didn't bother.

This rule change had a large and positive impact on how people made investing decisions. According to data compiled by Shaton, changing the feedback given to households—making the timescale longer—led to much better investing decisions. They traded far less (which is almost always a wise approach to long-term investing) and seem to have taken smarter risks.

The same logic applies in nonfinancial domains as well. As demonstrated by the classic research of Solomon Asch, the urge to conform is a powerful human tendency, and can lead people to change their mind about even obvious facts. (In Asch's experiments, subjects exposed to errant answers from a group typically altered their answer to fit those of the group at least once, even if they knew the answer was wrong.[19]) Given the surfeit of feedback on screens—just look at all the comments underneath a typical Facebook post—I can't help but wonder if conformity is yet another example of a psychological principle that's getting amplified on screens, and not in a good way. We are more likely to be influenced by the crowd because the crowd is harder to avoid. Even when we're alone we're still only a swipe away from learning about the opinions of others.

Look, for instance, at a recent study by Swiss researchers that investigated the impact of feedback from "friends" on social media.[20] Christian Hildebrand, a psychologist at the University of St. Gallen, was inspired by various shopping Web sites, such as Nike.com and Lego.com, that encourage customers to share their custom-designed purchases on Facebook, Twitter, Instagram, and Pinterest. (Many of these sites offer coupons and rewards to customers who share.) Hildebrand wanted to know how all this sharing affected consumer choices and consumer satisfaction. Did the feedback from friends and strangers make us happier about our purchase? Were we more pleased with our new running shoes and Legos?

The answer was a resounding no. In one study, conducted in collaboration with a car manufacturer, Hildebrand looked at how feedback on social media influenced the kind of car people chose. In general, he says, customers who heard back from other people tended to pick cars and options (such as exterior color) that were far less distinctive. Instead of buying the bright yellow roadster, they settled for the gray sedan. They conformed to the crowd.

Alas, this conformity has a real cost; when it comes to the amount of feedback we receive from friends on our purchases, even a little bit of feedback is probably too much. In a second experiment, Hildebrand and colleagues invented an online tool for designing jewelry. They also built a special platform for sharing these designs with others. In the first experiment, more than one thousand women were asked to create a pair of earrings. After giving the women feedback about their earrings—the feedback was purportedly from another community member—the scientists found that the women, like those car buyers, tended to revise their choices in line with the comments. Over time, these revisions caused them to be much less satisfied with the end result. In another follow-up study, Hildebrand actually built the earrings as designed. A few weeks later, the scientists called the women and offered to buy the earrings back. Those who had received feedback had worn their earrings only about half as much as those who hadn't. They also requested an average buy-back price of 14 Swiss francs, which was less than half what those who received no feedback requested. "Our results show that feedback dampens creativity, reduces originality and diminishes customer satisfaction," Hildebrand and colleagues write.[21] And yet, despite these results, companies continue to encourage their customers to share their purchases on social media. The problem with sharing, of course, is that people then tell us what they think. This feedback doesn't make us smarter or lead to better decisions—it just makes us less happy with what we've already bought.

Not every wall needs a mirror.

THE ANONYMOUS SCREEN

It was a call that many academics used to dread: an editor at an academic journal asking you to review someone else's paper. While such peer reviews are obviously necessary, they're also time-consuming and unpaid. (It's a bit like jury duty—somebody needs to do it, but you don't always want to be that somebody.) However, the personal nature of the call—an editor was on the phone, making a one-on-one request—made it hard to say no, at least for me.

But now the system works very differently. Instead of phone calls, most journals send automated e-mails from a Web site, which ask you to agree to review a manuscript. At first glance, this system might seem more efficient; e-mails are faster than telephone calls; the same written request can be used again and again. Unfortunately for academic journals, these e-mails are also far easier to decline. I might feel guilty saying no to an editor I respect if he or she is on the phone, but clicking "decline" is a little emotionally easier. (I do, of course, agree to review all the papers I can manage, as modern science depends on the peer-review process.) And this isn't just my reaction: I've talked to journal editors who tell me that since the new e-mail system was put in place, the percentage of academics who decline review requests has skyrocketed. It's becoming a big problem for the academic community.

What the journals have learned the hard way is that the medium of the request—whether we're asked by a human or on a screen—leads to very different reactions. For example, if a friend tells me to read a particular book, I'll typically thank him for the recommendation, even if I'm not that interested. But if Amazon suggests a book, I have no qualms about telling the computer it's wrong, and that I almost certainly won't like it. I'm not shy about telling the machine what I really think because it's *just a machine*—it won't be offended, or think less of me. At a dinner party, I would never tell the host I didn't like his food, even if that was the truth. Yelp, however, is filled with furious reviews, as people vent their anger to a screen.

These differences in behavior are driven by the nature of screens. It turns out that computers feel *anonymous*: while we care about the feedback we get from humans, we know that machines are just a bundle of microchips and wires, running a code of zeros and ones. As a result, we're less concerned about the feedback given to us by screens; their impersonal nature makes the advice easier to shrug off.

Such anonymity cuts both ways; you probably won't be surprised to learn that it's sometimes good and sometimes bad. Let's start with the good. It turns out that people are far more honest when interacting with a screen instead of a person. (The negative reviews on Yelp, TripAdvisor, and other ratings sites are evidence of this phenomenon.) This is known as the disinhibition effect, and it's often triggered by the presence of technology. According to the psychologist Adam Joinson at the University of the West of England, screens can lead to disinhibition because they remove the normal feelings of anxiety and self-consciousness that exist when we are judged by another person. Joinson outlines the varied evidence for online disinhibition, how it influences our behavior in everything from Web journals—people can be extremely confessional, even in public forums—to online pornography, which features far more "exotic" content than its nondigital competition.[22] It even affects how students respond when receiving feedback about a written essay, as those who receive feedback from a computer engage in more revision and rewriting than those who receive feedback from a human instructor. Because the students don't feel threatened or insulted by the computer's critical comments—it's just a mindless machine—they are able to reflect, without getting defensive, on what they'd done wrong.[23] And then they can fix it.

However, the most important consequences of the disinhibition effect almost certainly occur in the doctor's office. As Joinson notes, patients asked about their health via "computer-aided self interviews"—they fill out questionnaires on a computer screen—tend to report "more health-related problems and more drug use" than do those asked by a human being. They also showed signs of being more truthful, as men reported having fewer sexual partners and women reported having more.[24] (This corrected a long-recognized gender discrepancy in the number of reported sexual partners.)

Or look at the research of Fred Conrad, a cognitive psychologist at the University of Michigan. A few years ago, he decided to see how people responded to questions about their drinking habits when asked on a screen, instead of by a nurse or doctor. He recruited six hundred iPhone users, randomly assigning them to different conditions. Some of the subjects were asked by a human voice how often they binged on alcohol, while others were asked via text message on their phones. A clear pattern soon emerged: when the format of the questions was a text on a screen, people gave far more candid answers, with a third more people admitting to binge drinking in the last thirty days.[25] In short, people seem willing to confess to an anonymous machine what they'd never tell a medical professional.

This research comes with some obvious applications. Take alcohol consumption. According to a 2014 paper by Mandy Stahre and colleagues at the Centers for Disease Control,[26] excessive drinking is responsible for roughly 10 percent of all potential life lost among working-age adults in the United States, shortening the lives of those it kills by roughly thirty years. All of this booze comes with a huge price tag: the CDC estimates that excessive drinking costs the United States more than $200 billion per year.

How to solve this health crisis? The first hurdle is figuring out who has a problem. Philip Cook, a professor of public policy at Duke University, points out that the top 10 percent of drinkers consume over half of all the alcohol drunk in a given year.[27] (These heavy drinkers average more than seventy drinks a week, which works out to nearly two bottles of wine, or more than ten beers, *every day*.)[28] Unfortunately, many heavy drinkers lie about their levels of alcohol consumption, which makes preventive treatment very difficult. As a result, doctors rarely intervene until it's too late; the damage has already been done.

Here's where the disinhibition effect might prove useful. Instead of having doctors ask patients about their bad habits, we should have computers ask the questions. (Doctors might also prefer this setup, as many report feeling uncomfortable when prying into the lives of their patients.) The data suggests that such an approach would generate much more honest answers, which will help doctors identify those people who most need medical treatment. And it's not just drinking—related research has shown that computer interviews increase disclosure for a variety of risky health behaviors.[29] When dealing with sensitive subjects, the absence of human feedback—an absence made easy in an age of screens and machines—can be a great advantage.

Now for the bad news. While anonymous devices seem to make us more honest, they also lead us to indulge in irresponsible behaviors. The Internet is overrun with the by-products of these behaviors, which is why people leave so many nasty comments on blog posts: one study of a news site found that 22 percent of all comments contained incivility of some kind.[30] These are acts most of us would never commit if we knew someone else was watching—we wouldn't walk up to a stranger and tell them they were big fat idiots—and yet people do these things online all the time.

Here's another negative implication of screen anonymity, which has much bigger implications than rude blog comments. In recent years, many chain restaurants have introduced screen-based menus, so that customers order food and drinks from gadgets instead of people. (In 2014, Chili's and Applebee's announced the installation of nearly 150,000 tablets in their restaurants.[31] McDonald's, meanwhile, is currently conducting field tests in its franchises, allowing people to order food in advance through the McDonald's app.) For the restaurant chains, the devices offer clear advantages, increasing the productivity of their staff and minimizing the possibility of human error.

However, it's important to remember that screens are not neutral conveyors of information. Rather, they often alter the ways in which we respond to the message, creating unintended ripple effects that we need to consider in advance. Take those screens in restaurants. McDonald's might assume that customers ordering off their phones will order the same sorts of food as people telling a cashier what they want. But they'd be wrong. When we order food from a screen—when the feedback of the human staff is taken out of the equation—our preferences are shifted in predictable ways.[32]

Unfortunately, these shifts are bad for our health. A team of scientists—Avi Goldfarb, Ryan McDevitt, Sampsa Samila, and Brian Silverman—analyzed more than 160,000 orders placed over four years at a large franchised pizza chain. Because the chain introduced an online ordering system in the midst of the study period, the researchers were able to conduct a field experiment into how the introduction of technology changed the content of customer orders. According to the data, online customers chose pizzas that were more complicated and expensive, containing 33 percent more toppings and 6 percent more calories. Instead of just ordering a pepperoni pizza, they chose pies that featured highly unusual toppings, such as "quadruple bacon" or ham, pineapple, and mushroom. (When orders were placed online, bacon sales increased by 20 percent.) While such orders reflect our idiosyncratic preferences—the economists argue that online customers end up more satisfied, with a higher level of consumer surplus—they're clearly not good for our diets. We might want a pizza smothered in bacon, but our arteries definitely don't.

Why do people order less healthy food on screens? Goldfarb and colleagues believe that the phenomenon is driven by "online disinhibition effect," as we're less worried about what other people will think of our unhealthy order. (Previous research has found that subjects eat fewer calories when they think a scientist is keeping track of their food intake, and that people are more likely to leave food on the plate in the presence of others.)[33] In other words, because the screens offer us little feedback—gadgets don't judge—we feel free to indulge our least responsible desires.

And it's not just food. In recent years, the anonymity of screens has also changed the kind of culture people consume. *Fifty Shades of Grey* is an erotic romance novel about sexual bondage. Released in 2012, the book became a surprising smash hit, selling more than 100 million copies in less than three years.[34] How did such a racy book become a best-seller? Technology played a huge role. At its peak, *Fifty Shades of Grey* was selling six times more e-books than print copies.[35] The appeal of the digital version is obvious, as its readers didn't have to endure the scorn of a clerk at the bookstore, or the judgment of strangers if they read the book in public. Only their e-reader knew they were actually immersed in erotica.

There is, of course, nothing wrong with a little racy fiction. However, as we make more and more choices online, it's important to think about the ways in which our choices might be influenced by the lack of human feedback. It's good when we tell the truth to our doctors. It's bad when that truth involves admitting that we like to eat pizza smothered in bacon.

THE SEVEN HABITS OF EFFECTIVE DIGITAL FEEDBACK

As I was finishing this chapter, I took my family to Israel for a month-long stay. Our timing was not ideal—shortly after we arrived, violence broke out between Israel and Hamas militants in the Gaza strip. The militants began launching dozens of missiles into Israel every day, and Israeli fighter jets responded by targeting missile factories and Hamas military leaders. What we imagined as a fun summer beach vacation was soon interrupted by a procession of air-raid sirens and sprints to the local bomb shelter.

I grew up in Israel, so this wasn't a novel experience for me—I've heard the same sirens several times before. However, I was soon struck by the ways in which technology has changed the experience of being under attack. (Some might call me naive, but I do hope Israelis and Palestinians will live peacefully and focus their technological efforts on economic prosperity.) The biggest change for my family has been the existence of a smartphone app called Red Alert that uses real-time information from the Israeli Defense Forces to warn people even if they can't hear the sirens. In many instances, the phone alert goes off first, giving Red Alert users a precious few extra seconds of warning to seek shelter. During the violent summer of 2014, the app was downloaded nearly a million times. To put this number in perspective, there are about five million Israelis living within the danger zone.

At first glance, Red Alert probably seems like a clear improvement over the old-fashioned air-raid siren. Who wouldn't want to know about a missile attack as soon as possible? And yet, as I spent more time with the app, I came to wonder about the effectiveness of its feedback, and whether or not the app was making a stressful experience even worse. There were many days and nights when, buzzing phone in hand, I found myself wishing I'd never downloaded the app in the first place.

In other words, Red Alert is a perfect illustration of both the promise and peril of all our new digital feedback. It's a reminder that, while the app represents a tremendous opportunity—those extra seconds can save lives—we also need to ensure that its information is effective and exists in accordance with the literature on human nature. Because bad feedback isn't just a waste of pixels and bandwidth—it can actually do harm. In this section, I want to outline seven basic principles that define high-quality digital feedback. My list is not exhaustive, of course—as more research is conducted, new principles will emerge. But these are a few of the ideas that came to me as I was anxiously staring at my phone in the bomb shelter, wondering where the missiles would fall next.

1. Time It Right

There are so many design variables of digital feedback that it's easy to forget that one of the important factors isn't visual at all—it's timing. Given the abundance of information competing for our attention, feedback has to arrive at the right time in order to have an impact.

Just consider Red Alert: the entire function of the app involves the speed of its feedback, its ability to deliver a warning before a rocket returns to earth. In fact, the speed of digital feedback is perhaps it's greatest advantage. For the first time, we can deliver feedback about behavior as soon as it happens; relevant information can always be on demand, delivered without delay. The days of the monthly bank statement, or the news flash that happens *after* the missile hits, are long gone.

If done properly, this just-in-time feedback can prove enormously effective. Take financial education. Although classes that try to teach people about the best ways to spend and invest their money are often incredibly ineffective—one metareview found that even twenty-four hours of classes didn't lead to enduring benefits[36]—education that is delivered at the precise moment the consumer is making a pertinent financial decision can be quite useful. (This is known as "just in time" financial education.) That, at least, is what we learned from our field study with Personal Capital. As research from the Federal Reserve demonstrates, consumers often use digital devices to get financial feedback. Furthermore, this feedback allows them to exert far more self-control over their spending decisions, as they refrain from buying things they can't afford. And while the intuitive design of Personal Capital certainly helped, the biggest breakthrough is its timing. When it comes to using feedback to alter people's behavior, we have a very limited temporal window—if it's not there when people need it, then it probably won't work.

2. Make It Personal

The Red Alert app allows users to personalize the location of their missile warnings. For example, I can choose which neighborhoods of Tel Aviv I want to know about. But there's a problem with this setup—it isn't automated. The app doesn't keep track of my location, which means that I have to tell the app, in advance, where I'm going to be. If I go to Jerusalem for the day, the app won't be useful unless I manually change the settings. And if I drive around Tel Aviv doing errands, then I have to continually update my location preferences.

I think this is a major missed opportunity. After all, one of the main advantages of digital feedback is the ease with which it can automatically customize our information, analyzing the data and passing along only the relevant bits. (See chapter 6 for more on this.) I have many apps that automatically track my location, from Yahoo! Weather to Waze—I'd be more likely to rely on Red Alert if it did the same thing. The best feedback begins with effortless measurement, with devices so subtle we forget we're even being watched.

3. Avoid Feedback Overdose

During the first ten days of hostilities in July 2014, Hamas launched more than 1,200 missiles into Israeli airspace. Almost all of them were shot down or fell harmlessly into uninhabited areas. However, because the Red Alert app didn't automatically personalize their locations, many users of the app received alerts for the entire country. As a result, each of these missiles generated a swell of buzzing phones and collective anxiety. One Red Alert user told *The Daily Beast* that "every time a rocket was launched, my phone went haywire. I finally had to get rid of it [the app]. It was driving me nuts." Another user confessed that the app "paralyzed" her with fear. "It wouldn't stop beeping," she said, "and quite frankly I didn't need to be reminded of how things were every minute of every day."[37]

I understand their complaints. In the interest of ensuring that no missile alert is missed, the designers of the app ended up inundating users with too much information about potential missile strikes. And when people receive too much feedback—when you end up on the right side of the inverted U-curve—it quickly becomes yet another source of background noise. A similar problem afflicts the Nike FuelBand, which is always telling me to be more active, regardless of how many steps I've already taken. As a result, I've learned to ignore all of its recommendations, even when I should listen. In an age of information overload and scarce attention, we're not looking for devices that simply give us more feedback, or track everything about our lives. We're looking for screens and gadgets that cut through the clutter, that tell us more with less.

4. Trigger a Feeling

In 2002, the psychologist Paul Slovic and colleagues gave a new name to an old idea. The idea itself is pretty simple: As Slovic pointed out, countless studies had shown that the brain was drawn to any information that came attached with emotion. It didn't even matter if the emotion was good or bad—we paid attention to whatever made us feel *something*.[38] Slovic called this the "affect heuristic."

This mental shortcut has important implications for feedback, because it suggests that we'll be more likely to notice feedback laden with emotion. (We'll also be more likely to alter our future behavior.) Just look at the Awesome Blossom deep-fried onion dish, which used to be served at Chili's restaurants. It was routinely cited as one of the unhealthiest appetizers in the world—a single dish contained 2,710 calories, 203 grams of fat, and 6,360 milligrams of sodium. Nevertheless, the Awesome Blossom remained extremely popular, even after Chili's added nutritional information to its menu.

How is that possible? Why would people knowingly order such a ridiculously unhealthy dish?[39] Duke psychologist John Payne suggests that one of the problems was that the caloric feedback didn't make people feel anything; the numbers by themselves generated little emotional response, which made them easy to ignore. (This also explains why simply providing calorie information on fast-food menus seems to have little impact.)[40] However, if we made it easier for people to figure out whether something is good or bad—whether the information was laden with emotion—then we might be able to fix the problem. For instance, would you still order the Awesome Blossom if you knew that you'd have to walk nine hours to burn off all those calories? Or that the dish contained the equivalent amount of fat of fifty slices of bacon? I'm guessing you'd order something else instead, since that feedback packs a bigger emotional wallop.

The digital world opens up new possibilities for using the principle of affective ease. The GlowCap, for instance, is a pill bottle top that reminds people to take their medications. The simple product has a lofty aim—reducing patient noncompliance, which is a polite way of referring to people's not following the instructions of their doctors. Poor compliance is a massive problem: only about half of patients take their medications for chronic conditions as prescribed, which dramatically increases health care costs.[41] It's estimated that roughly 10 percent of all hospital admissions are caused directly by patients *not* following the pharmaceutical instructions.[42]

The GlowCap works like this: After a patient fills a prescription, the Internet-connected plastic top automatically downloads his or her prescription details.[43] Let's say, for instance, that you're suffering from high blood pressure and have been prescribed a medication to be taken twice a day, starting at seven a.m. After the clock strikes seven, the GlowCap begins emitting an orange light. If the pill bottle isn't opened within a few minutes, then the GlowCap starts to emit a ring tone as well. As the minutes pass, the tones grow louder and more insistent. (David Rose, the inventor of the GlowCap, refers to this process as one of "escalating reminders."[44]) This will continue for another two hours. If the pill bottle still isn't opened, then the GlowCap will send an alert to its servers, followed by an automated e-mail and text to the patient.

This system of gradual escalation—making sure that the tone of the feedback reflects the urgency of the situation—seems to be quite effective, at least for helping people take their medications. Because the GlowCap steadily raises the emotional stakes (a light becomes a flash, which becomes an annoying beep, which leads to an urgent text), patients are responsive to its reminders. In an experiment led by researchers at Partners HealthCare and Harvard Medical School, a control group of patients on high blood pressure medications took their pills as prescribed only about half of the time. However, those given the GlowCap were far more dutiful, and had a compliance rate above 98 percent.[45]

The Red Alert app could learn a thing or two from these escalating reminders. While the basic feedback of the app is obviously full of emotion—every time the beep sounds I know *exactly* how to feel—it could use more gradations, since not every attack is equally dangerous. In Tel Aviv, I have ninety seconds to respond to a beep. In Ashdod, farther south, I would have only fifteen seconds. Sometimes, the missiles are headed right toward me, while other missiles might be a few miles off. The tenor of the alert should express the urgency of the situation and take advantage of our ability to respond to subtle differences in emotional feedback. If it did, I'd be more likely to listen.

5. Incorporate an Action Plan

I've been critical of the Red Alert app, but it's important to note that it's only a first iteration, and is bound to improve. In fact, the Israeli government recently announced that they are working on their own app, which will not only warn people about incoming missiles, but also give them personalized instructions on what to do during an attack. For instance, if you're walking in an unfamiliar location and hear the sirens, the app will give you directions to the nearest shelter.[46]

I think these changes would represent a huge improvement. That's for a simple reason—feedback is far more effective when it comes attached with some actionable instructions. A recent study led by David Nickerson at the University of Notre Dame found that simply calling voters and encouraging them to vote did not increase turnout. *At all.* However, if people were asked when and where they planned to vote—such conversations led to the formation of a voting plan—then they were nearly ten percentage points more likely to vote in the election. (This effect existed only among single-eligible-voter households.) In short, encouraging people—even with a personal call—wasn't enough. Instead, what mattered was offering feedback that got voters to think, in the most practical terms, about how to achieve their desired outcome.[47]

Of course, such instructions are far easier to generate in the digital world. We no longer have to create driving directions by hand, or send reminders one at a time. If there's one thing algorithms are really good at, it's finding a way to get us from Point A to Point B, telling us how to close the gap between where we are and where we want to be. Sometimes, that will be an urgent set of directions to the nearest bomb shelter. And sometimes it will be a plan suggesting that we stop by a local voting center during our lunch break, because our phone already knows when we're free.

6. Encourage, Don't Criticize

One of the interesting psychological questions confronted by every designer of digital feedback is how to deal with people who don't listen. Should we offer gentle criticism, reminding them that they ate the wrong foods, or didn't take nearly enough steps? Or should we ignore their poor performance? In other words, how honest should we be?

I don't think these questions have clear answers, at least not yet. In general, the scientific literature emphasizes the importance of positive feedback, since encouragement tends to increase a person's belief that his or her goal can be accomplished.[48] We can lose those pounds; we can exercise more; we can find ways to spend less money. (Positive feedback is especially useful among novices, who are still gaining confidence.) However, if a little negative feedback is necessary—and sometimes there is no way around it—then I think it's important to deliver it in the right way. As always, digital feedback works only if it reflects the tendencies and traits of the human mind.

The most important feature of useful negative feedback is making it about the task, and not the person. Consider a recent study of seventy-one cardiothoracic surgeons who were learning how to use a new technology for heart surgery.[49] The scientists were particularly interested in how the surgeons learned from their inevitable mistakes and failures. Did it make them better surgeons, more likely to succeed with the next patient?

Unfortunately, the answer was frequently no—their errors were not as educational as they should have been. Instead of grappling with their mistakes, the surgeons seemed to blame external factors beyond their control, which inhibited their future progress. However, there was a very interesting pattern hidden in the results. It turned out that doctors saw big boosts in their own success rates when they watched a *colleague* fail at the new surgery. In other words, they were good at learning from the screwups of others, and terrible at learning from their own screwups.

This has clear implications for digital feedback. It reveals just how defensive people get after a mistake, how loath we are to take responsibility. And that's why we should keep our negative feedback gentle and future oriented, focused on the task and not the user. The goal is not assessing blame—it's providing people with specific instructions so they can do better the next time around.

I was thinking about this while struggling with the Red Alert app. As the days went by, I came to dread all of its chimes and beeps. On the one hand, this is entirely predictable: the app is designed to give me only bad news, to alert me when explosives are falling from the sky. And yet, I think the app could be even more effective if it utilized some of these insights into the importance of balancing positive and negative feedback.

For instance, one of the uncertainties of an air-raid siren involves knowing when it's safe to come out. (Shrapnel from an intercepted missile can take a few minutes to fall back to earth.) If I were designing the Red Alert app, I would build in a reassuring alert to let users know they're now safe. This bit of good news at the end of an attack would accomplish two things: (1) it would ensure that people didn't leave their shelter too soon; and (2) it would give them emotional closure on the event, diminishing the chronic anxiety that comes from being under attack. Sometimes, negative feedback is necessary. But if it's the only thing you're offering—if you're always telling people to walk more, or eat less, or run for their lives—then they're going to tire of the process eventually.

7. Follow the Evidence

I hope this chapter has demonstrated the surprising ways in which human beings react to digital feedback. In the age of screens, we have an unprecedented opportunity to learn about the impact of our behavior, to get constant updates on ways we can do better. However, this opportunity is no guarantee of success, as even the best-intentioned systems can go astray. And that's why all digital feedback must be thoroughly tested. We need to identify our sweet spot on the inverted U-curve, but we should also experiment with the style and tenor of feedback, continually altering the design of these new mirrors. We need to get feedback on our feedback.

ASK YOURSELF

I've got a weak spot for acrostics, those mnemonic devices in which the first letter in each line spells out a word. They've always been a useful memory compression device for me, helping my brain recall a complex process with a single cue. Below, I've recast my seven behavioral principles as an acrostic for the word DIGITAL.

Dosage: Are you delivering too much feedback? Don't become noise.

I: Are you making personalization easy? Mirrors should be effortless.

Good: Is your feedback too negative? If so, look for opportunities to offer up positive suggestions.

Intuitive: Are you taking advantage of the affect heuristic? We are intuitively drawn to information that triggers an emotion.

Timing: Are you delivering your feedback at the most effective possible moment?

Actionable: Do people know how to react to your feedback? Does it come with a plan for improvement?

Learning: Are you measuring the outcome of your feedback? Is it improving behavior? Never underestimate the uncertainty involved when trying to change human behavior.

CHAPTER 5

———

Desirable Difficulty

THE AGE OF PIXELS

In 1985, at the dawn of the computer age, the psychologist Susan Belmore conducted a simple experiment on twenty undergraduates at the University of Kentucky.[1] The students were exposed to eight different short texts and then asked to answer a series of questions about what they'd just read. Four of the passages appeared on paper (a sheet of white bond, single-spaced, forty-seven characters per line) and four appeared on the monitor of an Apple II Plus 48k computer. Belmore was curious if reading the text on a screen might influence both the speed of reading and levels of comprehension.

The results were depressing, at least if you were an early adopter of computer technology. "These data indicate that reading texts on a computer display is not equivalent to reading the same texts on paper," Belmore wrote. "Overall, college students took 12 percent longer to read and comprehended 47 percent less with computer-presented text than with paper-presented text." Think, for a moment, about what this means: not only did the students read more slowly on screens, but they understood roughly half as much of what they were reading.

What caused this effect? Belmore blamed the users' lack of experience with screens and machines. Because people weren't used to reading on computers, they were distracted from the text, unable to focus on the words. Instead of thinking about the reading material, they fixated on the flickering monitors and pixelated fonts.

In the years following Belmore's experiment, psychologists continued to find nagging differences in how people read on paper and on computers. In the mid-1980s, J. D. Gould and his colleagues at IBM began an exhaustive investigation of these differences. After replicating Belmore's basic finding—people read worse when reading on screens—the IBM scientists analyzed a long list of potential explanations. They eventually concluded that the phenomenon was driven by a multitude of seemingly insignificant visual factors, most of which were caused by low display resolution.[2] As the psychologist Andrew Dillon noted in a 1992 review article based, in part, on Gould's research, "Invariably it is the quality of the image presented to the reader which is crucial . . . Until screen standards are raised sufficiently these differences [between paper and screen] are likely to remain."[3]

Such research suggests that there is nothing inherently wrong with computers. Rather, the problem is the poor quality of the display; paper was better only because screens had yet to catch up. In fact, Gould demonstrated that if a monitor could approximate the clarity of printed text then the discrepancies in reading comprehension would disappear.

Needless to say, the quality of computer monitors has improved at a dramatic pace. The monochrome displays have given way to screens capable of displaying 16.8 million colors; the latest iMac desktop now features eighty times the number of pixels as the original

Apple Macintosh. (In 1984, the best monitors featured 175,000 pixels—now, they feature nearly fifteen million.)[4] Designers have even begun tinkering with the text itself, inventing custom fonts tailored for LCD and e-ink displays. (Amazon.com, for instance, brags that its Kindle fonts have been "hand-tuned at the pixel level.") Such tweaks are rooted in an obvious concern: if a site isn't easy on the eyes, then people just might look away.

Given this stunning progress, one might expect digital reading to have leapfrogged paper reading. Perhaps we now read *better* on screens, as their stunning clarity makes reading even easier. After all, the latest iPhone model now features more dots per inch—401 DPI on the iPhone 6 Plus—than the finest printed books, which are closer to 300 DPI. If reading comprehension is a function of visual ease, then we should be reading on these "super screens" at unprecedented levels. We should remember more than ever before.

But that hasn't happened—the dramatically improved quality of screens has not led to higher levels of comprehension. If anything, the opposite seems to have occurred. Consider a 2013 experiment led by Anne Mangen, a Norwegian psychologist at the National Center for Reading Education and Research. Her experiment had a straightforward design, a deliberate attempt to replicate previous studies on reading and screens.[5] (The research was motivated, at least in part, by planned changes to Norway's standardized testing system, in which texts will appear on computers, and not as printed documents.) Seventy-two tenth graders were randomly assigned to one of two groups. In the first group, the readings were handed out on paper, printed in 14-point Times New Roman font. In the second group, the same texts were distributed as PDF files, with the students reading them on fifteen-inch LCD monitors featuring 1280×1024 resolution. After they finished reading, all of the students completed a series of questions designed to test their level of reading comprehension.

The results were sobering. It didn't matter what text the students were given—they always comprehended less of it when they read it on a computer. "The results of this study indicate that reading linear narrative and expository texts on a computer screen leads to poorer reading comprehension than reading the same texts on paper," Mangen wrote. While she didn't pretend to fully understand the causes of this effect— she speculated that a lack of "spatiotemporal markers" on screen leads to worse reading comprehension—Mangen found the effect to be significant and consistent. As she points out, even small differences in test performance can have big consequences. For instance, a student who misses a few additional reading comprehension questions on the SAT— perhaps because he or she is taking the test on a screen instead of on paper—would see a drop in his or her total verbal score. This suggests that as standardized tests transition to computer screens, the creators will need to recalibrate their scoring algorithm since students will perform worse on computers. (The ACT is currently piloting a digital version, while the SAT is launching their digital version in 2016.)

The persistence of the digital reading gap, even in an age of gorgeous LCD displays, is a remarkable finding. For decades, scientists assumed that the quality of the display was the essential variable when it came to reading comprehension; it was the constraint on our learning. And yet, we now have screens that are no longer inferior to paper—and are often *better* than paper, at least in terms of image quality—and the digital reading gap continues to exist.

This chapter is about our online reading problem, but it's also about some possible solutions. Because this is a problem that needs to be solved: screens allow us to read more than ever before, but they also encourage us to read poorly, and to remember less of what we read. If you want people to engage with your content—and to really learn from it—then you need to understand the cause of the digital reading gap, which turns out to be quite unexpected.

THE DOWNSIDE OF EASY

Why are computers still worse for reading, despite the tremendous progress in screen quality? Here's my speculative explanation: the quality of the screens is still the problem. Only now the problem is that these super screens are *too good*, at least compared with paper. Although the initial studies blamed the poor quality of the monitors for the digital reading gap—they made reading excessively difficult—I now think the current generation of LCD screens makes reading *too easy*; the brain doesn't work hard enough.[6] The end result is that we fail to fully process the words on the screen. *Easy in, easy out.*

Isn't ease supposed to be a good thing? After all, behavioral economists have spent years demonstrating the clear relationship between making something easy to do and getting people to actually do it. My very good friend and longtime collaborator Richard Thaler puts it this way: "My number-one mantra from *Nudge* [his book, cowritten with Cass Sunstein, on the application of behavioral economic principles to public policy] is, 'Make it easy.' When I say make it easy, what I mean is, if you want to get somebody to do something, make it easy. If you want to get people to eat healthier foods, then put healthier foods in the cafeteria, and make them easier to find, and make them taste better. So in every meeting I say, 'Make it easy.' It's kind of obvious, but it's also easy to miss."[7]

Thaler is absolutely right: the benefits of ease should not be under-estimated. Easy Web sites make consumers more likely to engage with the content; making things easy also makes people far more likely to complete transactions. This helps explain why Amazon patented the one-click buying system and the best e-commerce sites autofill relevant information, such as our billing address and e-mail. In one study, only 3 percent of customers who attempted to buy something on their smartphone actually made the purchase. The authors of the study speculate that this dismal completion rate was due, in part, to a lack of autofill on mobile devices.[8] In short, it wasn't easy to spend money.

One of my favorite examples of the "Make it easy" mantra comes from a recent study looking at prospective college students applying for student loans. As you might expect, the loan application forms are tedious and complex, especially for an eighteen-year-old. To make this process easier, the U.S. government partnered with H&R Block to create software capable of automatically filling in about a third of the application based on available family tax returns. This simple intervention came with impressive results, at least for the students in the study. After H&R Block made the forms easier to complete, students were 39 percent more likely to submit a loan application. Even more impressive, receiving help with the autofill on the application increased college enrollment among graduating high school seniors by almost 30 percent.[9]

But (and this is a big *but*) making things easier is not always ideal. In particular, when it comes to learning and memory—the very skills measured in tests of reading comprehension—excessive ease has serious drawbacks. Sometimes, people actually remember more when the information is slightly harder to process; the perceptual struggle is a good thing. To understand why easy can be problematic (and hard can be the solution), it helps to know about a series of clever experiments led by Connor Diemand-Yauman, Daniel Oppenheimer, and Erikka Vaughan. In a highly cited 2011 paper published in *Cognition*, the scientists showed that making material *harder* to read—what the researchers call *disfluency*—can actually improve long-term retention.[10] To give you a sense of what these experiments were like, I'd like to run a quick one on you. I am going to provide you with specific facts about two alien species, the pangerish and the norgletti. Please read the following lists.

The pangerish:	The norgletti:
• Ten feet tall	• Two feet tall
• Eats green, leafy vegetables	• Eats flower petals and pollen
• Has blue eyes	• Has brown eyes
• Webbed feet	• Distinct toes
• Eight fingers	• Four fingers
• Sleeps for twelve hours	• Sleeps for four hours
• Orange hair	• Yellow hair

Are you done reading? Now please get a glass of water, take two sips, and then turn the page.

I'm going to ask you a few questions about the alien species. This is a test of memory, so don't look at the list of facts. Write down your answers in the space provided.

How tall are the norgletti?

What color eyes do the pangerish have?

What is the diet of the norgletti?

How tall are the pangerish?

What is the hair color of the norgletti?

How many fingers do the pangerish have?

Do the norgletti have webbed feet?

What is the hair color of the pangerish?

Now please go back and check your answers. Obviously, this is an extremely small sample, so we're not going to get significant results— I simply want to help you understand how scientists are studying the effects of fluency. You might not have noticed it at first, but the different alien lists were printed in different fonts. (The pangerish were described in **Comic Sans** while the norgletti were described in Arial.) Did the different fonts affect your memory?

When the psychologists ran an extended version of this study on twenty-eight undergraduates at Princeton University, they found that those students exposed to disfluent fonts—they used 12-point **Comic Sans MS** in 60 percent grayscale or 12-point Bodoni MT 60 percent—performed better than those given the information in pure black Arial. While subjects in the fluent condition correctly answered 72.8 percent of the questions about the fictional creatures, those forced to read disfluent fonts correctly answered, on average, 86.5 percent of the questions. (There were no significant differences between the different disfluent fonts; both Comic Sans and Bodoni were equally effective at increasing the retention of the reading material.) Ugliness has its advantages.

Of course, this cute experiment comes with several important limitations. For one thing, the short duration of the study doesn't reflect the reality of the classroom, in which students must remember material for longer than a few minutes. It's also possible that the benefits of disfluency might disappear in a real-world setting. There's probably a reason this book isn't printed in **Comic Sans**.

To address these concerns, the scientists set up a second experiment involving actual students in a public high school in Chesterfield, Ohio. They began by getting supplementary classroom material, such as PowerPoint presentations and worksheets, from a variety of teachers. (Subjects included English, physics, U.S. history, and chemistry.) Then, the researchers changed the fonts on all of the materials, transforming the text with a variety of disfluent fonts, including *Monotype Corsiva*, **Comic Sans Italicized**, and **Haettenschweiler**. Because all of the teachers included in the study taught at least two sections of the same class, the psychologists were able to conduct a carefully controlled experiment. One group of students was given the classroom materials with the disfluent fonts, while the other group was taught with the usual mixture of **Helvetica** and **Arial**.

After several weeks of instruction, the students were then tested on their retention of the material. In nearly every class, the students in the disfluent condition performed significantly better than those in the fluent condition. (The sole exception was chemistry, for reasons that remain unclear.) "This study demonstrated that student retention of material across a wide range of subjects (science and humanities classes) and difficulty levels (regular, Honors, and Advanced

Placement) can be significantly improved in naturalistic settings by presenting reading material in a format that is slightly harder to read," write the scientists. "Fluency demonstrates how **small interventions** have the potential to make big improvements in the performance of our students and education system as a whole."

It's important to note that there's nothing magical about **Comic Sans** or **Haettenschweiler**. While some fonts are objectively more difficult to read—perhaps there is less spacing between the letters, or the letters themselves are less differentiated—the main reason most fonts are disfluent is simple: we are less used to them. They are less familiar. For example, my default font is Calibri. By now, I am so used to the look of Calibri that any other font (even Times New Roman) slows me down. I have little doubt that if **Comic Sans** were my default typography, then it would cease to be disfluent. I would no longer read it more carefully, and the educational benefits of its silly typeface would disappear. The only long-term solution is to engage in a form of "dynamic disfluency," switching up my digital typefaces so my brain never gets too fluent at reading any particular font. The irony, of course, is that all of these tricks are necessary to simply create a reading environment on screens that's as effective as the ancient technology of paper.

THE UPSIDE OF HARD

Why does disfluency lead to more learning? Oppenheimer refers to the ugly fonts as a "desirable difficulty," noting that multiple studies have shown that increasing disfluency leads subjects to process information more carefully. Instead of just reading the text, they are forced to think about it. The speedy mind—and remember that people might think even faster on screens—is made to slow down. As a result, people engage with the material at a deeper level.

Consider a series of recent experiments led by Adam Alter, a psychologist at NYU. In his research, Alter relied on a well-known assessment called the Cognitive Reflection Test, or CRT, pioneered by the psychologist Shane Frederick.[11] The short test is designed to measure the extent to which an individual relies on mental shortcuts and quick instincts, giving subjects tricky questions in which their initial hunch is almost always incorrect. Here's a classic question from the CRT: "A bat and ball cost $1.10 in total. The bat costs $1 more than the ball. How much does the ball cost?" The intuitive response is that the ball costs ten cents. That, however, is incorrect: the ball actually costs five cents. (The bat costs $1.05, for a total of $1.10.) When Alter gave people the CRT in a disfluent font—he used a small print in a very light gray—they were far less likely to get the wrong answer.[12] While 90 percent of subjects in the fluent condition got at least one of the CRT questions wrong, only 35 percent did so in the disfluent group. In short, the hard-to-read text forced subjects to think more deeply about the questions, which led them to get far higher scores.

It's worth pointing out, however, that not every study looking at disfluent fonts gets similar results. For reasons that remain unclear, many experiments have found little to no effect when counterintuitive math problems, such as those in the CRT, are printed in hard-to-read letters. While people take longer to answer the questions, this extra time doesn't lead to higher scores. Clearly, more research is needed.[13]

In a separate experiment, Alter and colleagues made up a user review of a new MP3 player. When the headline of the review was printed in an easy-to-read font, subjects tended to focus on superficial aspects, such as the look of the reviewer. However, when the headline was printed in a disfluent font people were far more likely to make a judgment based on the substantive content of the review.[14] The takeaway, says Alter, is that exposing people to disfluent information increases the likelihood that they will engage in more deliberate thinking strategies. "When something is difficult, that should act as a meta-cognitive alarm or a signal that you don't understand it as well as you perhaps should," Alter said in a 2013 interview.[15] The feeling of disfluency, then, isn't just an annoyance or inconvenience— it's actually a crucial mental signal, telling us to slow down and focus. It's a reminder that we need to think more.

Such a signal has enormous practical application. I've often wondered, for instance, why the surgeon general's warning on packs of cigarettes is printed in easy-to-read fonts, such as Helvetica. Given the research on disfluency, wouldn't it make more sense to print the ominous warnings ("Smoking kills," etc.) in Comic Sans? Don't we want consumers to notice and reflect on the medical advice? If so, then we should make the warnings *harder* to read, not easier.

Or consider a mortgage application. In recent years, the government has devoted an incredible amount of effort to regulating the layout of information on loan documents. (Rules mandated by the Dodd-Frank Act devote more than eight hundred pages describing the disclosures required when consumers are "applying for and closing on a mortgage loan.") Interestingly, one of the requirements of these new federal regulations is that all relevant information be written in an "easily readable type font," and for important notices to be "no smaller than 12-point size."[16]

This is obviously a well-intentioned rule; the Consumer Financial Protection Bureau wants to make sure that the most important details, such as the interest rate or length of the loan, aren't hidden from consumers, buried amid the avalanche of fine print. And yet, it's interesting to think of this requirement in light of the fluency effect. Given the extra cognitive reflection associated with disfluent fonts, wouldn't it make more sense to require lenders to highlight the most important information in a *difficult*-to-read format? If the goal is to get people to really think about whether or not they should take out a particular mortgage, then it seems like consumers would be better off with the *Monotype Corsiva* font.

And this returns us to the digital world. Given the impressive technical progress of the last few decades, digital information has become far easier to process: it has strengthened the effects of fluency. While that ease can often be a good thing, the relentless push for fluency has also made people *less* likely to remember and retain what they read. Instead of thinking carefully about the information on our super screens, we are more likely to skim and forget. (You're probably more likely to finish a book on your iPad Air, but you're also less likely to remember what you read.)

But the fluency effect isn't just about reading comprehension—it also seems to interfere with the way we learn, especially when taking notes. Look, for instance, at a recent study from Pam Mueller and Daniel Oppenheimer.[17] As Mueller and Oppenheimer observe, it's increasingly common for students to write down material on laptops and tablets; the keyboard is replacing the pen. While this transition comes with numerous benefits—people tend to type much faster than they write, and the typed notes are easier to search—several studies have found that laptop note taking is less effective for learning. The typical explanation is that laptops encourage distraction, allowing students to check their e-mail during lectures and waste time on Facebook during class.

Mueller and Oppenheimer, however, wondered if the appealing ease of computer note taking was responsible for the decreased learning. And so, in three separate experiments, they showed students video lectures on a wide variety of topics. (Some of the talks were taken from the TED Web site; others were technical videos about bread, respiration, and vaccines.) Half of the students were randomly allowed to take notes on the laptop—all other applications had been disabled to prevent distraction—while the other half took notes on an old-fashioned pad of paper.

The first thing the scientists found is that students randomly assigned to the laptop note-taking condition were far more likely to take "verbatim" notes on the lecture. According to Mueller and Oppenheimer, they did this because they were able to keep up with the speed of speech. In contrast, students taking longhand notes were forced to summarize the content as they listened along; they had to choose what to remember. The end result is that they engaged with the material at a deeper level, encoding the information before writing it down.

Such encoding comes with major benefits. Across all three experiments, Mueller and Oppenheimer found that the "pen is mightier than the keyboard," for reasons related to fluency. What's more, this advantage existed even when subjects were given time to study their lecture notes. Although those in the laptop condition had far more written material to look over, the students who had taken notes by hand scored much higher on tests of factual learning and conceptual learning. Mueller and Oppenheimer conclude that the slowness of handwriting is yet another "desirable difficulty," a source of disfluency that leads to improved educational outcomes. Based on the data, they argue that "laptop use in classrooms should be viewed with a healthy dose of caution; despite their growing popularity, lap-tops may be doing more harm in classrooms than good."

We're only beginning to grasp the implications of the fluency effect, especially as it shapes thinking in the digital age. One study I often think about was done by Linda Henkel, a psychologist at Fair-field University. Henkel asked subjects to photograph various paint-ings in a museum. The next day, she gave them quizzes about the artwork. She quickly discovered that those who took snapshots with their digital cameras were far less likely to remember the details of the paintings, at least when compared with those who only observed the art.[18] Henkel refers to this as the "photo-taking-impairment effect." "People so often whip out their cameras almost mindlessly to capture a moment," Henkel told the Association for Psychological Science, "to the point that they are missing what is happening right in front of them."[19]

But Henkel also discovered a simple way to minimize the photo-taking-impairment effect. When subjects were asked to zoom in on a particular detail of the painting, they preserved their memory of the entire artwork, including details that were out of the frame of the photo. I think disfluency helps to explain what was going on. Instead of simply taking a snapshot of the entire canvas, subjects were forced to slow down and focus on a particular element of it. This made the process slightly more difficult, just like taking notes by hand, but that's precisely why the subjects remembered more of what they'd seen.

PRESCRIBING A DIFFICULTY DOSAGE

The takeaway from all this research is that cognitive ease comes with trade-offs. Instead of assuming that easy is always good, we should begin by considering our goal. Do we want customers to complete the transaction? Finish the text? If so, then we should maximize their perceptual and cognitive fluency. We should autofill as much as possible and rely on the Helvetica family of fonts.

Take a recent study done at the MIT AgeLab. The scientists were interested in how various typefaces on a car's dashboard screen influenced driver performance. After testing eighty-two adult subjects in a driving simulation, they found that so-called humanist typefaces—these are generally regarded as easier to read, due to their wide spacing and "highly distinguishable shapes"—reduced the amount of time drivers had to look away from the road by 10.6 percent. (The effect was particularly pronounced among male drivers, for reasons that remain unclear.) The more fluent humanist fonts also reduced the error input rate by 3.1 percentage points, meaning that drivers were less likely to have to turn away from the road again. This suggests that, when it comes to the dashboard design of cars, the most fluent fonts are best, as they minimize distractions.[20]

But high levels of fluency, as should be clear by now, are not ideal in every situation. That's why, if we want people to actually remember what they read, then we should seriously consider deploying a little disfluency. It's not about being carelessly ugly: it's about getting the mind to slow down, to actually process all the words on the screen. Sometimes, this might be best accomplished with DESDEMONA, or perhaps some *Schoolhouse Cursive* or Papyrus Condensed. But an unfamiliar font is merely the tip of the iceberg; there's no need to restrict ourselves to the design variable relied upon by experimental psychologists. When it comes to disfluent designs, anything that makes perception less automatic—whether it's a hint of grayscale or an unexpected layout—will also lead to more cognitive reflection. We won't just read what's on the screen. We might actually think about it and remember it.

How could disfluency be used in practice? The crucial principle is to find the right dosage of difficulty, to hit the peak of the inverted U. If the dosage is too high—if customers have to work too hard—then they won't bother engaging; the site will be a total turnoff. However, if the dosage is too low, and the site is too fluent, then they might not remember what they read in the first place. As any doctor will tell you, too much medicine can be just as harmful as not enough.

The same principles can be extended to virtually all aspects of Web design. Take, for instance, a start-up like Uber, which connects people looking for rides with local cars for hire. For the most part, the Uber Web site and app are a model of sleek fluency. They feature a high-contrast black screen, offset by white text boxes; everything is printed in a legible humanist font, except for the UBER logo. The app even brags about its "one tap to ride" feature.

This is all excellent design, since Uber's main goal is to make it as easy as possible for people to call a ride. However, once a customer opens an account, and begins booking cars, things get a little more complicated. At this point, Uber has to explain to people how the service actually works. In particular, it has to make sure they understand the principles of surge pricing.

What's surge pricing? When demand for drivers is high—say, during a blizzard, or on New Year's Eve—Uber uses an algorithm to raise its rates so more drivers will sign on to the site and start picking up passengers. As I mentioned in the introduction, this sometimes leads to extremely high surcharges: when a snowstorm blanketed Manhattan in December 2013, Uber charged some customers 8.25

times the normal fare, which led to accusations of price gouging and mobs of angry customers on social media. This suggests that many of Uber's most loyal customers don't understand its basic business model.

The first thing to note is that an 8.25 multiple is almost certainly too high. As Thaler said, in a survey conducted by the Chicago Booth IGM Forum, "people care about fairness as much as efficiency,"[21] and $415 for a cab ride just seems unfair. But even if Uber capped its pricing multiples—and I think it should—it would still have the problem of customers' being surprised at the total cost. In a sense, the very fluency of the site can backfire, because many customers don't fully process the surge pricing warning. (It probably doesn't help that surge pricing sometimes goes into effect late at night, when many Uber customers have had one too many drinks.) To deal with this problem, Uber instituted a separate screen that forced customers to acknowledge its pricing mechanism: before the car was called, the customer had to click "I agree" after being told about the expected fare increase. However, even that warning didn't seem to work, as every bad storm still generated a flurry of negative feedback. As a result, Uber was forced to enter a new stage of disfluency: when the surge pricing multiple is over 2.0, it now forces customers to type in the exact amount of the multiple (e.g., "8.25×") before they can hail a car.[22] This is an extreme example of disfluency—it deliberately makes it harder for people to complete a transaction—but it just might keep Twitter from lighting up with furious Uber customers after the next snowstorm.

Uber's long-term success requires that customers grasp its pricing model. In other words, it's not just a taxi company—it's also in the education business, teaching users the logic of supply and demand and Econ 101. Given the research on disfluency, Uber should continue to experiment with new ways of helping people make sense of surge pricing. Visual disfluency, such as changing font types, is an obvious approach—one that is easy to fine-tune with A/B testing. I believe, however, that Uber should also experiment with *cognitive* disfluency, which involves making people think more about the information, as in the case of having to actively type in the surcharge multiple. Has Uber reached the optimal difficulty dosage? Perhaps, but if customers continue to be confused about what the surge multiple actually means—I wonder if some people think it's more akin to a percentage tax—then Uber should boost its disfluency dosage and make passengers engage a bit more with the math. One possible strategy is to have Uber clients manually do the arithmetic calculation, as they multiply the base cost of their ride times that surge multiple. The numbers just might slow us down long enough to make us think twice about using the ride service and thus avoid a choice we will soon come to regret.

There is a larger lesson here. For too long, we've assumed that the ideal form is always fluent, but that's not the case. The best design is not about making it as easy as possible on the eyes. Rather, it's about balancing the demands for cognitive ease with the benefits of desirable difficulty; the craving for speed with the benefits of slowing us down. If used properly, disfluency is not about turning people off—it's about making them notice what they'd normally skim over, using visual cues to encourage them to think more deeply about the material on the screen. The form of information should serve its ultimate goal. Easy is good, but sometimes hard is even better.

ASK YOURSELF

The digital world tends to assume that high levels of fluency are always better—when in doubt, make it easy. But the psychological literature suggests that the deliberate use of disfluency can actually be quite helpful, at least when it comes to making us think more carefully about what's on the screen.

1. Before you decide on the ideal level of fluency, it's important to establish the goal of your digital information.

    a. Do you want people to complete a transaction or make a quick purchase? If so, then high levels of fluency are ideal. Make the process as easy as possible.

    b. Do you want people to remember what they read, as in a classroom? If so, then introduce a measure of disfluency to the content. Find ways to slow the mind down.

    c. Do you want people to reflect on the information, as in the case of mortgage rates or cigarette warnings? This also calls for a level of disfluency.

2. Are you leveraging the different types of disfluency?

    a. Have you been using visual disfluency? You might begin with font changes—try using unfamiliar typefaces—but should also consider new layouts. Find ways to make the eyes work a little bit harder.

b. Have you considered cognitive disfluency? Examples include using "fancy words," as my five-year-old, Maya, calls them, or forcing users to manually enter information, as in the case of Uber and surge pricing.

3. Have you prescribed the right dosage of disfluency? The balance is essential, as excessive ease might not grab attention, but too much difficulty can turn people away. Use A/B testing to identify the proper dose of disfluency. In addition, eye-tracking data might help pinpoint places where disfluency can be introduced to boost attention and reflection. Focus on the part of the screen that the eyes skim over.

CHAPTER 6

———

Digital Tailoring

THE POWER OF PERSONALIZATION

Every morning, I get my daily fix of caffeine at the same place. It's a simple café a few blocks from my campus office. They make the best cappuccino in town. But I don't show up here every day just for the quality of the coffee. Rather, it's the quality of their customer service that earns my loyalty. It begins before I walk in the door: the baristas recognize my car, so as soon as I pull up they start pulling my shot. They also know that I prefer my cappuccino in their old white mugs, which are only five ounces. (The new mugs are eight ounces—too much foam.) Last, they let me order half of a croissant—the owner eats the other half—which is good for my diet. It's seven in the morning and I'm still half asleep. But I already feel a little special. Not a bad way to start the day.

This is a mundane example of personalized customer service: the baristas know what I like and cater to my particular preferences. You probably have your own examples, whether it's a clerk at the dry cleaner's who remembers how you want your shirt collars, or a sales-person at your favorite clothing store who gives you a call whenever they get your favorite jeans in stock. It's hard to resist such service, which is why even big companies, such as Starbucks and Burger King, promote their own attempts at personalization. (Starbucks encourages customers to create their own "signature" drinks, while Burger King urges people to "Be Your Way.") In a world of automated everything, there's something extremely gratifying about getting a little one-on-one attention.

In recent years, scientists have begun to measure the benefits of personalized service, both for customers and for those serving the customers. Consider this experiment, which was conducted at a restaurant in Ithaca, New York.[1] The team of scientists, led by David Strohmetz at Monmouth University, wanted to understand the variables that influence the size of a tip. They began by having the staff offer "each person in the dining party a fancy, foil wrapped piece of chocolate" when delivering the check. As expected, the strategy proved reasonably effective: when each customer was given a single candy, the average tip increased by about two percentage points.

However, the psychologists soon discovered a far more powerful approach. After offering the customers the same selection of chocolate bars, the waiters were instructed to turn and leave, as if they were moving on to a new table. But then, after a few steps, they suddenly turned back around, looked the customer directly in the eye, and said that he or she had been such a good guest that one chocolate bar wasn't enough. The customers were then offered a second bar.

The results were dramatic. When the wait staff didn't offer any chocolates to their customers, the total amount of tips offered during the experiment was just over a thousand dollars. However, after the second chocolate bar was combined with a seemingly spontaneous offer, the size of tips surged to $1,235.75. What's more, this represented a significant increase over an experimental condition in which customers were offered two chocolate bars at the start. The lesson, say the scientists, is clear: personalized gestures can increase tip size, regardless of "the actual quality of the service provided during the party's dining experience."

Why is personalization so effective? One of the main reasons is that it makes us more attentive, increasing our awareness of that free chocolate bar. In a world saturated with generic content, personalized gestures find a way to cut through the clutter. We notice information and actions when they've been designed just for us.

These gains in attention can lead to major benefits, as demonstrated in a study by the psychologists Diana Cordova and Mark Lepper.[2] Their experiment revolved around a math video game given to fourth- and fifth-grade students. The game wasn't particularly fun, as it asked the students to solve a long series of arithmetic problems. In the control group, the students received a generic set of instructions at the beginning of the game:

It's July 28, 2088. Planet Earth is facing the worst energy crisis in history. As Commander of the U.S. Space Fleet, your mission— as well as that of your crew—is to travel 3 trillion miles to Planet Ektar in search of titanium, a highly powerful source of energy. All necessary supplies are being loaded into the spaceship's cargo compartment. Best of luck in your journey, Commander.

In the "personalized" condition, however, the students read instructions that had been specifically written for them based on their responses to short questionnaires:

It's [the child's birthday], 2088. Planet Earth is facing the worst energy crisis in history. As Commander of the U.S. Space Fleet, your mission—and that of your crew—Mission Specialists _____, _____, _____ [three of the child's closest friends], is to travel 3 trillion miles to Planet Ektar in search of titanium, a highly powerful source of energy. All necessary supplies, including _____, _____, and _____ [names of the child's favorite foods and/or toys], are being loaded into the spaceship's cargo compartment. Best of luck in your journey, Commander _____ [child's nickname].

These customized instructions—a rudimentary example of digital tailoring—significantly influenced how the students responded to the video game. When the instructions were *not* personalized, students gave the game an average score of 2.9 on a 1-to-7 scale of enjoyment. In contrast, when the same game began with a personalized introduction, they gave the game an average score of 5.42. They were also nearly twice as likely to stay after class in order to play the game. All this extra pleasure came with big benefits, as students in the personalized condition scored more than 30 percent higher on a subsequent math test.

According to Cordova and Lepper, personalization enhances our attention and enjoyment for two reasons. The first reason is that it increases levels of intrinsic motivation. Because the information seems "self-relevant"—the students understood how it related to them—they were willing to invest the extra effort required to solve harder math problems. The second reason involves a factor known as "perceived competence," as subjects exposed to personalized information are more convinced that they can excel at the game. This, in turn, makes them more likely to persevere. As the researchers note, the same logic should apply to any complicated information processing task. Unless the content has been personalized, then we probably won't notice it. We save our scarce attention for the stuff that feels the most relevant.

Of course, once our attention has been grabbed, it's far easier to influence our behavior. (We can't act on information we don't perceive.) That, at least, is the lesson learned by hotel chains. For the last fifteen years, most major chains have been trying to persuade their guests to reuse their towels, thus saving water, detergent, and labor costs. You've probably noticed the strategically placed placard in your hotel bathroom, asking you to hang up those towels you'd like to use again. The savings are potentially significant: if the majority of guests at a typical hotel reused their towels, each hotel would save more than seventy thousand gallons of water every year.[3] That's roughly equivalent to the amount of water in three hotel pools.

Alas, the well-intentioned placards don't seem to be very effective. According to a recent study led by Noah Goldstein, a psychologist now at UCLA, placards with the "standard environmental message" work only about a third of the time.[4] However, Goldstein also discovered a simple trick to make them more persuasive. After testing various possibilities, Goldstein found that the most personalized messages worked best. For instance, when people were told that the majority of other guests staying at the hotel had reused their towels, they were about 26 percent more likely to do the same. However, when they were told that the majority of guests staying in their particular room had reused their towels—each placard was customized for its room location—participation in the program increased by about 33 percent. Goldstein explains the results by noting that people are far more likely to follow a prosocial norm, such as saving water, when the norm is expressed in terms of their "physically proximate surroundings." The more proximate and personal, the better.

So personalization is persuasive. In study after study, messages tailored to the individual—and it doesn't matter if the tailoring involves personal information, location, or timing—are far more effective at garnering attention and triggering behavior change. It's a truth that every good barista and salesperson already knows, but now we have the data to prove it.

This chapter is about how the digital world is dramatically expanding the possibilities of personalization, giving us new opportunities to connect with people on an individual level. The first new opportunity involves scale: by taking advantage of smart software and algorithms rooted in Big Data, it's possible to customize information for millions of people for very little money. While personalization in the real world comes with obvious expenses—better customer service requires more employees—this trade-off doesn't exist in the digital world. Once you write the code, it's nearly as expensive to personalize the experience of ten people as it is to personalize the experience of ten million.

Look, for instance, at an interactive ad campaign I saw on a recent trip to Israel. A few years before, Coke had introduced its "Share a Coke" campaign, in which consumers were able to personalize cans and bottles of Coca-Cola Classic with their first names. The campaign has been widely credited with boosting sales, as consumers share their "personalized" labels on social media. (Every tweet is a free advertisement for the soft drink.) However, I was most struck by an experimental campaign conducted on several highways around Tel Aviv. The campaign featured an electronic billboard and a location-based

Coca-Cola app for mobile phones. As users approached the outdoor ad, they received a message notifying them about the billboard: for a few thrilling seconds, the billboard spelled out their name in bright lights. It's an admittedly superficial gesture, but it still led to more than 100,000 downloads of the Israeli Coke app in a few weeks.[5] By personalizing the billboards, Coke got people to engage with the brand to an unprecedented degree. Just as those students paid more attention to the math computer game when it featured their first name, so were the drivers more attentive to the Coke billboard when it was addressed to them. The only difference is the number of people involved: while the scientists had to manually program the game for each student, the Coca-Cola app did everything automatically, reaching thousands of people at no additional cost.

But digital personalization is not just about economies of scale. That's how the tool has been mostly used online, but I think that's only a first step. In fact, I think the real potential of personalization involves the ways it can be combined with other strategies to create a novel kind of nudge, unique to the world of screens. In this chapter, we'll explore a variety of new techniques, from altered self-portraits to customized videos, that make people more likely to engage with important material. By leveraging the insights of behavioral science, it's possible to personalize the impersonal screen.

VISUAL PERSONALIZATION

The online world is a visual place; screens emphasize the act of looking. This is partly because screens are a technology geared toward the eyes, a flat surface we stare at. But it's also a by-product of information overload, as the sheer quantity of content coming our way means we can keep up only by scanning the display, our eyes searching for the most relevant facts. We might be thinking faster than ever before, which means we are "thinking" more and more with our eyes.

This helps explain why I'm so excited about new personalization techniques that take advantage of visualization technologies. In its most basic form, this approach uses customized pictures to cut through the clutter. It's premised on the assumption that visuals are an information-compression device, allowing us to transmit more content and emotion in less space and with fewer words. Just look at a simple strategy employed by the Behavioural Insights Team, which is also known as the Nudge Unit of 10 Downing Street. Established in the summer of 2010, the team consists of a small group of behavioral economists attempting to apply academic insights to British public policy with the ultimate goal of encouraging people to make better choices for themselves.[6]

Recently, the Behavioural Insights Team began altering the letter sent to British citizens if they failed to pay taxes on their car. The traditional letter was all text, informing the subject that if they didn't pay now they would be hit with various penalties, including a clamped car and hefty fines. To increase the effectiveness of the letter, the scientists began experimenting with various forms of personalization. The first variant involved making a more specific threat, telling recipients that they would lose their particular model of car if they didn't pay the tax. The second variant featured a personalized visual, so that the letter came attached with a photograph of the actual car in question. While both approaches increased compliance, the customized picture was the most effective—it increased the compliance rate from 40 to 49 percent.[7]

This is a good start, but I think we might be able to do even better. What would happen, for instance, if the Behavioural Insights Team began digitally altering the photograph? Would even more people pay their taxes if the letter included a picture of the car model in question being *towed*? I know that would get my attention.

A similar approach could be used in countless situations. For instance, you can download a free app called AgingBooth on your smartphone. By using digital photo editing effects, the app automatically ages your selfies, inserting wrinkles, saggy skin, and tightened lips. When you look at your portrait in AgingBooth, you are put in touch with your future self—you might feel your creaky bones and hunched posture, or marvel at all those new lines around your eyes. An abstract concept—*I will get old*—gives way to a more visceral awareness.

Such awareness, it turns out, can have a large impact on our subsequent decisions. Consider the research of Hal Hershfield, one of my colleagues at UCLA. In a study published in 2011, Hershfield and colleagues used virtual reality technology to personalize the self-portraits of subjects.[8] After putting on special goggles, they were asked to look at themselves in a virtual mirror. Here's where things get interesting: the mirror contained a picture of the subject, except this picture had been digitally manipulated to make the college-age student appear seventy years old. They had been given gray hair and mottled skin; their face was covered in wrinkles.

This brief encounter with their aged reflection changed how people planned for their future. After looking at their digitally manipulated portrait for sixty seconds, the subjects were then asked to allocate $1,000 among four different options: they could buy something nice for someone else, invest it in a retirement fund, plan a fun occasion, or put it into a checking account. Hershfield and his collaborators found that people exposed to their aged reflection allocated more than twice as much money to a retirement fund ($172 versus $80) than participants exposed to a picture of their current self. In another lab experiment, Hershfield demonstrated that this approach could be easily implemented online, as participants who uploaded their own headshots said they would save approximately 40 percent more money after looking at a rendering of their older self.

Why do we act like this? Hershfield argues that people tend to feel "disconnected from their future self."[9] This disconnect helps explain why we sometimes do irresponsible things, whether it's eat unhealthy foods (even though we know these foods will make us feel ill tomorrow) or fail to save enough for retirement. However, Hershfield's simple visualization tool diminished this sense of detachment; the future self became a more vivid presence. The end result was a sudden shift in decision making, as subjects exposed to an image of their aged face acted in ways more in line with their long-term interests.

Hershfield's research demonstrates the far-reaching effects of digital personalization, especially when combined with new visualization tools. Too often, the future is an abstract entity with remote consequences. As a result, we recklessly discount it, and give in to the temptation of immediate gratification. However, by combining personalization and visualization, Hershfield has shown that our tendency to neglect the future can be partially overcome. Although we all know we *should* save for the future—the majority of Americans admit they aren't saving enough[10]—it isn't until we're shown a customized picture of our future selves that we start acting in a more responsible manner.

A similar technique could be used in myriad ways. Hal Hershfield,

Dan Goldstein, and I are currently conducting a field study that tries to figure out if exposing people to an aged picture of themselves when checking their 401(k) accounts online can increase savings in a real-world setting, and not just in the lab. In a second study, Hershfield and Goldstein are looking at whether or not body visualizations can decrease weight gain among long-haul truckers. For instance, if a subject gained five pounds last week, the scientists would send them an image of their body in six months if the current trend persists. (Such pictures are rarely flattering.) Not surprisingly, truckers tend to suffer from severe weight issues, as their job gives them little time for exercise and makes them reliant on a diet of fast food. Hopefully, providing truckers with a visual reminder of the need to eat healthily can help them develop better eating habits. They will become more aware that indulging in the present has tangible consequences.

We're only beginning to explore the potential of personalized visuals. One of the possibilities I find most exciting involves customized videos, in which the content and narrative of a short clip is tailored to each viewer. One of my good friends, Danny Kalish, is the cofounder of Idomoo.com, a start-up that has pioneered the development of such videos. (Disclaimer: I'm on the academic advisory board of the company.) Kalish got the idea for Idomoo after noticing that most people rarely have time to read anything, let alone unpack a complicated piece of content. "We're all so distracted now that if it's longer than a text [message], you're probably not going to look at it," he says. "So what's the best way to transfer information? I thought, video is good, but video isn't enough. We've got to make it personal, too."[11]

Such digital personalization marks a turning point in the communication of information. For decades, there were two fundamentally different ways to inform and influence people. On the one hand, there was the impersonal broadcast route, which included everything from television commercials to online banner ads. Such broadcasts had tremendous reach—you could expose millions of people to the same message—but they were also expensive and easy to ignore. (New technologies, such as the DVR, have made it even easier to tune out ads.) On the other hand, Kalish says, there was the one-on-one approach, which featured a trained employee interacting with a customer. This personalized approach was far more effective, but could not scale without becoming prohibitively expensive. "The beauty of personalized video," says Kalish, "is that you can combine the best of these strategies. You get the scale of broadcast"—he likes to refer to Idomoo as an automated video factory—"and a success rate that compares to one-on-one conversation."

In one recent video, Idomoo turned a typical electrical utility statement into a ninety-six-second video that delivered the same basic information in a far more personalized manner. The customers were still told about their usage, except now the numbers were read aloud while customized graphics of a house flashed across the screen. In addition, the video made a clear social comparison, showing how their own energy consumption compared with the usage of their neighbors.[12] "Before you can convince people to save energy, you have to grab their attention," Kalish says. "And given all the other stuff out there, it helps to be as personalized as possible."

Kalish then rattles off a list of successful Idomoo case studies. There's the personalized video for a bank that led to a sevenfold increase in loan applications; the how-to installation video for a Brazilian mobile phone company that led to a 9 percent decrease in the number of unsuccessful installations; the explanatory video for a large cable company that triggered a 30 percent reduction in service center calls. According to Kalish, these customized videos get results because they imitate the personalization of the best customer service interactions. "In every phase of the video, I can decide what is the best story to tell you," he says. "I can predict what you'll actually care about." As Kalish notes, such personalization is something that we all do naturally in conversation, as we continually adjust the content of our speech to fit the interests of the other person. "It's the most human thing in the world," he says. "It's just that computers have never been able to do it before. Now they can. And they can do it with massive scale."

Kalish describes how this process works for those electric utility customers. "If you use too much energy, then we're going to tell you a very different story than someone who has already replaced their light bulbs or put in more insulation," he says. "If you've always paid on time, then I don't need to tell you about late fees." In other words, digital personalization enables a far more effective transmission of information, allowing organizations to highlight the most relevant facts in a short amount of time. In an age of scarce attention, when the typical Web site features pop-up ads, video commercials, and multiple banner billboards, it's more important than ever to tailor the message to each and every member of the audience.

It's not an accident that many of these new digital personalization examples involve visuals, such as self-portraits or short video clips. As Kalish likes to point out, it's hard to get people to consume large amounts of text; the online world is too full of distractions. And that's why interventions that feature tailored images and customized videos are often so effective. If a picture is worth a thousand words, then a personalized picture might be worth a thousand pictures.

And a personalized video might be worth many personalized pictures.

My hope for this research is that we find a way to use personalized visualizations to make more people aware of the consequences of their choices. I'm not suggesting that we make decisions for consumers or even take away any options—I simply want to remind them that Big Macs can lead to a big belly, and that our aged self will need some savings. People already know this, of course. I'm just trying to give this knowledge a newfound emotional power.

TIMING IS EVERYTHING

A good waiter has to have an impeccable sense of timing. The job, after all, requires that he or she must constantly interrupt the customer, barging in on conversations to announce the daily specials or offer dessert menus. As a result, it's important that these interruptions occur at the right moment, so that they don't feel so intrusive. If a group is engaged in an intense conversation, they probably don't want to order cocktails. If a couple is in the middle of a romantic kiss, then maybe their water glasses can be refilled later.

This is a personalization problem. Like those restaurant customers, we're incredibly sensitive to the timing of an appeal or offer. In fact, personalizing the timing of an interaction—making sure it occurs at the right moment—is nearly as important as tailoring the content. That's why sending the same message at different times of day, or on a different day of the month, can produce dramatically different results.

That, at least, is the conclusion of research led by Hengchen Dai, Katherine Milkman, and Jason Riis at the Wharton School.[13] In a series of recent experiments, the scientists have shown that people are significantly more likely to "tackle their goals," such as starting a diet or going to the gym, after reaching a "temporal landmark." They refer to this as "The Fresh Start Effect." The power of this effect is large: According to the data, the typical undergraduate is 33.4 percent more likely to work out on the first day of the week and 47.1 percent more likely to work out on the first day of the new semester. This even applies to our birthdays, with the probability of going to the gym increasing by 7.5 percent on the day after a celebration. (Not surprisingly, the scientists found that this pattern doesn't apply to our twenty-first birthday.)

As Milkman notes, her research has practical implications for the digital world, giving us yet another tool to personalize information and trigger the right kind of behavior change. When encouraging people to pursue their most aspirational goals, Milkman argues that we need to time our interventions, and that appeals to our better self—that part of us that wants to lose weight, save money, and go to the gym—will be far more effective if we make them at the right moment. Instead of asking people to start a diet on a random Tuesday, we should ask them on the first day of the month or right after a big birthday. Katherine Milkman, John Beshears, Hengchen Dai, and I are now working with half a dozen large universities to encourage employees to save more for retirement. Some employees are sent a mailing offering them the opportunity to increase their savings rate after a personalized landmark, such as a birthday. Other employees are offered the opportunity to increase their savings rate after an equivalent time delay, but without the personalized frame. The preliminary results suggest a significantly higher savings rates for those who are invited to save more around a birthday.

Another example of the power of personalized timing comes from the Behavioural Insights Team. One of their latest experiments is the Stoptober campaign, an online effort run by Public Health England that tries to get people to quit smoking cigarettes.[14] To figure out which Web sites were most effective, the Behavioural Insights Team and Public Health England conducted a randomized study that looked at the effect of various design permutations. For instance, one design displayed a bright orange "carousel" at the top of the Web page, featuring the campaign slogan: "Stoptober, it's like October but without the cigarettes." Another design featured a testimonial—"I quit 11 months ago and I just feel so proud of myself"—while another combined a testimonial with a picture of a middle-aged woman.

Not surprisingly, these different designs had a significant impact on the percentage of people registering for Stoptober. While the least effective designs signed up only 15.1 percent of Web site visitors, the most effective ones had a sign-up rate of 17.2 percent. (The single most effective template featured a testimonial about living ten years longer, with no photograph or carousel at the top.) This might not sound like a big effect, but given the scale of the campaign—it reached more than 939,000 people—it still led to some significant differences, with better designs leading to thousands more people committing to quit cigarettes.[15]

However, when the researchers and the economists at the Behavioural Insights Team began to analyze the data, they realized that the design of the site wasn't the only factor influencing the percentage of people who registered for Stoptober. It turned out that the *timing* of the Web site visit had a major impact, so that people visiting the Web site in the morning were 3.8 percent less likely to sign up when compared with other times of day. Mornings, however, didn't affect every Web site design equally. Instead, the morning seemed particularly hard on complex Web site designs, with each additional element reducing morning sign-ups by 0.3 percentage points.

What explains these results? It's not totally clear. But one likely possibility is that our attention is particularly scarce in the morning. There's just so much to do—we have to feed the kids and get them ready for school, catch up on e-mail, prepare for meetings, scan the news. As a result, we are easily overwhelmed by a Web site with too many features and too much information, which leads us to ignore the appeal. (MailChimp, a company that manages large e-mail campaigns, has data showing that people are more than twice as likely to open an e-mail at four p.m. than at nine a.m.)[16] By making sure that the form of the Web site was optimized for the time of day—and that morning appeals weren't too complicated—the researchers estimate that, for the next Stoptober campaign, they will be able to increase sign-ups by 5.9 percentage points. That's more than fifty-five thousand additional smokers deciding they need to quit.

So timing matters. These smokers almost certainly knew that cigarettes were bad for them. But unless the appeal to quit arrived at the precisely right time, and in the right form, it was far less effective campaign. I think a similar pattern applies to many different aspects of self-improvement, from going to the gym (as Katherine Milkman has demonstrated) to making better financial decisions. In a metareview published in 2014, Daniel Fernandes at the Catholic University of Portugal, John Lynch at the University of Colorado, and Richard Netemeyer at the University of Virginia looked at the effectiveness of financial education.[17] Their assessment was based on the results of 168 different scientific studies that looked at the impact of financial education. Long story short: the education didn't make a difference. In fact, even intensive classes involving more than twenty-four hours of education failed to improve the financial decision making of students two years later. If there was a benefit, it sure didn't last long.

Despite these dismal results, the scientists don't call for an end to financial education. Instead, they propose a form of "'just in time' financial education tied to [the] specific behaviors it intends to help." For instance, rather than teach people about mortgages in the abstract, we should give them important facts when they are applying for a home loan; rather than lecture about retirement savings at some arbitrary point in time, we should save it for when they are choosing a 401(k). In other words, if financial education is going to actually impact behavior, then the timing needs to be personalized. Obviously, the ubiquity of smartphones makes such "just in time" education far more feasible, allowing us to strengthen the impact of personalization. In theory, it's possible to text or e-mail people a little financial advice every time they are in danger of making a poor financial decision, whether it's taking out a subprime mortgage or withdrawing money from a savings account. At the very least, such personalized education can make them more aware of future consequences. As we learned in chapter 4, by providing users with a simple mobile app that provides real-time information about their spending, we can help them spend significantly less money on nonessential purchases. The information has a big impact because it's there when they need it.

All of these examples converge on the same takeaway: the effectiveness of Web sites, apps, and behavioral interventions is closely linked to their ability to personalize their information. This is why the most convincing hotel placards specify the room number, and the best learning software makes children feel as if the software has been customized just for them. It's why the personalized videos of Idomoo get such big results and why it's possible to get a significant jump in behavior change simply by sending out an e-mail at the right time of day.

The mind is very good at ignoring information. The potential of digital tailoring is to help us notice what we should already know.

THE BEST INVESTMENT

Perhaps the most remarkable aspect of these new personalization technologies is their cost effectiveness. While personalization in the offline world required significant payroll expenses—companies had to train and hire additional workers—digital personalization provides all of the same benefits (and maybe more) with few trade-offs. In fact, the initial evidence suggests that investing in digital personalization provides a massive return on investment (ROI). Coca-Cola, for instance, spent nearly $8 million just to buy airtime for its 2013 Super Bowl commercial.[18] I can't help but wonder if that ad budget would have been better spent using technology to connect with people on an individual level. If the point of advertising is to buy a few seconds of consumer attention, then you might get far more bang for your buck by personalizing the content.

Consider the experience of the Behavioural Insights Team. The initial goal of the team was to design interventions with an overall 10x return on investment. This meant that, for every pound the British government invested in the so-called Nudge Unit, they would get 10 pounds back, either as a reduction in needs (one intervention helped people transition off unemployment insurance) or as new revenue. While many politicians were skeptical about the team's potential, its first few years proved the skeptics wrong, as the Behavioural Insights Team averaged a 22x return on investment. (Over the next five years, their interventions are expected to save the British government more than 300 million pounds.)[19] However, the results from the Behavioural Insights Team's personalization interventions have been even more effective and, in at least one case, generated an ROI close to *2000x in a few months*.[20] Because many of the strategies used by the team were not digital—they involved things like writing by hand on a governmental form letter—it's reasonable to expect that the digital ROI might be even higher. After all, once a computer is programmed, it can personalize huge amounts of information at little additional cost. The old trade-off of personalized customer service—namely, that personalization requires more and better-trained employees—no longer exists. Thanks to impressive technological advances, it's now possible to reap the benefits of personalization without the cost.

Alas, the vast majority of governments and businesses have failed to take advantage of the full potential of personalization on screens. In too many instances, large amounts of information are transmitted in a generic form, leaving Web site visitors confused and unmotivated. People are unable to sort the most important facts—say, recent changes in their energy usage or the most relevant results in their medical lab results—from all the other information filling up the paper or screen. And so the pension statement is thrown into the recycling bin; the utility bill is unopened; the e-mail from our health care provider is deleted after little more than a glance.

There's no longer any excuse for such failures, as the available evidence clearly suggests that even minor attempts at personalization come with a huge ROI. Because we live in an age of digital personalization, it no longer takes significant resources to make customers feel special; the trade-off has been largely removed by technology. Sometimes, all it takes is an automatically produced video, in which a human-sounding voice says your name. Or perhaps a lesson plan that explains why this is the right lesson for you. Or maybe an altered picture of your own face, staring back at you from the future.

ASK YOURSELF

Personalization is one of the most important principles to keep in mind when providing information or offering choices to customers. The mind is an information-processing machine, but it is drawn to information that is tailored for its unique preferences, interests, history, and even location. (Web sites have a lot to learn from good waiters.) Here are a few questions to think about when trying to leverage the tools of digital personalization:

1. Are you using all the relevant data available to you? In particular, what do you know about your customers or clients and what can you do with it to personalize their experience? For instance, I'm a very frequent flier with United Airlines, and they could easily use my birthdate to send me a happy birthday e-mail. But they don't. Interestingly, another Star Alliance airline, Turkish Airlines, does remember my birthday, even though I fly with them far less frequently than with United. It's a little gesture—and it costs the airline nothing—but I remember it.

2. Have you considered the fine line between personalization and violations of privacy? It is important to set a balanced approach. Too much digital personalization can also come off as creepy.

3. Are you personalizing more than the content? For example, the timing of messages can play a big role in their effectiveness, which is why the Behavioural Insights Team personalizes the content based on the time a Web site is viewed. Similarly, how can you make the most out of temporal landmarks, such as New Year's Day or birthdays?

4. Are you leveraging new technologies to boost the effectiveness of personalization? Consider personalized videos as well as new visualization techniques. For example, people are willing to save more for retirement if they see a digital rendering of their older self.

5. Do you need more than one Web site? Should you, for example, consider a different Web site for the morning, evening, and late night? Or, should you set different Web sites for different clients, say a "quick" version for those with limited attention and a "deep" version for those who have more attention and interest in the topic?

6. Are you investing enough in digital personalization? Given the remarkable return on investment, should you spend more on personalization?

7. Are you aiming high enough with your digital personalization strategy? Our newfound ability to analyze huge amounts of data is enabling new forms of personalization. Amazon, for example, has filed a patent for an algorithm that allows the company to ship products before consumers even place their orders. That might seem crazy now, but it wasn't so long ago that we also would have laughed at the possibility of an algorithm telling us what movies we should watch.

CHAPTER 7

The Choice Opportunity

OBAMACARE

I began this book by discussing the launch of healthcare.gov, a shopping Web site designed to help millions of Americans choose the health insurance plan that best fits their needs. Unfortunately, the launch of healthcare.gov was a fiasco—according to several estimates, less than 1 percent of users were able to complete an application during the first week.[1] There were server failures and processing glitches; the Web site was a wreck for months. While these technical problems were eventually fixed—and more than eight million people were enrolled in 2014—the public relations damage was done. It's hard to think of a bigger digital disaster, or a more sobering reminder that Web sites are often a crucial element of effective public policy.

However, as I mentioned in the introduction, I think that the focus on the technological problems of Obamacare distracted us from asking a far more important set of questions. The goal of healthcare.gov, after all, was to help people make a difficult choice. Given the reach of the Web site, even seemingly minor design tweaks undoubtedly had a huge impact, influencing a key financial decision in the lives of millions of Americans.

So did healthcare.gov get it right? Did the site steer people to the best possible plan for their family? As I wrote earlier, there's evidence the Web site may have led to poor decisions, even after its technology was fixed. (We'll learn why later in the chapter.) The good news is that new research suggests ways in which the site can be improved in the future. Better design can lead to better decisions.

Let's begin by outlining the basic challenge faced by healthcare.gov: there are lots and lots of different health care plans. In fact, there were more than 78,000 distinct plans listed on federal and state health care exchanges. Even after various geographic and demographic filters were applied to the choice set—users were shown plans available only in their local insurance ratings area, for instance—people still had to deal with scores of alternatives. In Florida's Seminole County, for instance, there were eight different insurers, offering 169 different plans.[2]

To make matters worse, each of these health care plans differed in dozens of ways, from the family deductible to the co-pay for primary care visits. Each plan had different drug benefits and different charges for X-rays; different doctor networks and different overall quality ratings. All of these variables meant that visitors to health care.gov were given an overwhelming amount of information. They were asked to make a huge financial decision—the cheapest plan my family could enroll in was more than $600 per month—with little guidance or help. It shouldn't be too surprising, then, that so many online shoppers felt overwhelmed and confused.

Here, for instance, is a list of ten insurance options that appeared on healthcare.gov for the citizens of Seminole County. Keep in mind that I'm showing you less than 6 percent of the available plans, and leaving out many of the attributes listed on the Web site. (If you don't understand what all of the terms mean, don't feel bad: very few people do.) If I included the entire choice set and all of the variables, the list would take up about ten pages of this book.

So let's do a quick exercise. Please look at the health insurance options below and choose the plan that's best for you and your family.

	PREMIUM	DEDUCTIBLE	CO-PAY	CAT	TIER
1.	$392	$6,000	$40	EPO	BRONZE
2.	$464	$5,000	$25	HMO	PLATINUM
3.	$519	$3,000	$20	EPO	GOLD
4.	$562	$850	$15	EPO	PLATINUM
5.	$376	$6,000	$40	HMO	BRONZE
6.	$544	$0	$10	EPO	PLATINUM
7.	$189	$5,600	$10	HMO	BRONZE
8.	$240	$3,750	$10	HMO	SILVER
9.	$362	$5,750	$75	EPO	SILVER
10.	$378	$3,500	$30	PPO	SILVER

That was pretty hard, right? It's not at all clear which variable is most important, or even how the variables are related to one another. What's more, the ideal plan depends on your expected future health care needs—how many times will you go to the doctor next year?—which is not easy to predict. There's an awful lot to think about and very little guidance on how to do it.

Years of research have revealed what happens in these situations, where people are confounded by the size and complexity of a choice set—they don't choose anything at all. They give up. Just look at Medicare Part D, a government program that subsidizes the cost of prescription drugs. When the program was introduced in 2006, the government offered consumers more than a thousand distinct drug plans. However, in a study of people who decided *not* to enroll in Medicare Part D, 69 percent said there were too many alternatives and 61 percent said that the enrollment process was way too complicated.[3] As with healthcare.gov, the government assumed it was enough to offer people lots of options. But that's merely the first step. What happens next is just as important, for we need to give people a process that helps them narrow down the possibilities and choose a good one.

Of course, the problem of hard choices isn't an issue only for health insurance Web sites. Rather, it's a recurring theme of the digital age, as we make more and more choices on screens. We choose groceries on our phones and pick airplane seats on our computers; we buy and sell stocks while sitting on the couch and browse thousands of profiles on dating Web sites.

It's important to note that these new online choice environments are not simply mirrors of their real-world equivalents—Match.com is very different from meeting people at a bar, just as Amazon is not merely another bookstore. It probably won't surprise you to learn that the single biggest difference involves the sheer amount of choices, as Web sites are able to offer us far more options than their offline competitors. Because my local drugstore has limited shelf space, it stocks only six different diaper brands; diapers.com offers me more than fifty. My local supermarket contains about 220 different kinds of cold breakfast cereal; Amazon offers 1,841 varieties. And those are relatively small choice sets, at least by online standards. Zappos sells 28,584 different women's shoes. (Men are forced to make do with only 15,247 footwear alternatives.)[4] When I was growing up in Israel, there was only a single television channel; now we have servers in the cloud that offer us access to almost every show ever made at any time.

At first glance, this vast expansion of online choice might seem like a good thing, a mark of technological progress. Because we suddenly have access to so many options, we're free to find the best one, whether it's diapers or shoes or health insurance. According to traditional economic theory, the quantity of choice is supposed to be a good thing for everyone, since those who want more choice will benefit and those who don't can ignore the additional options. More alternatives should lead to more happiness, or at least more satisfied customers.

But this intuition is wrong; our new world of boundless choice is not helping us choose better. While too little choice is stifling, having too many choices can be paralyzing; our bounded brain is overwhelmed, and we end up picking badly or giving up. In a paper published in 2011, psychologists Barry Schwartz and Adam Grant argue that the relationship between the amount of consumer choice and consumer satisfaction is best represented by an inverted U-curve.[5] (We learned about inverted U-curves in the chapters on feedback and fluency, as too much feedback and fluency can be just as dangerous as not enough.) Take a simple study on pens led by Avni Shah and George Wolford, psychologists at Duke University and Dartmouth College, respectively.[6] The scientists found twenty different pen options, all of which cost between $1.89 and $2.39 and contained black ink. The subjects were told that the pens cost about $2, but that they could purchase any of them for a special discounted rate of $1.

Here's where things get interesting. At first glance, offering people more pens might seem like a good thing, since they can find the pen that best suits their needs. Some people like ballpoint pens, others prefer roller-balls, or just care about the texture of the grip. Sure enough, offering people more pens led to a higher percentage of people buying pens, at least at first. When only two pens were offered, 40 percent of students bought one. However, when there were ten pens to consider, 90 percent of people found one they liked enough to buy.

But now comes the inverted U-curve—when more than ten pens were offered, people became much less willing to choose any pen at all. The drop-off was steep: when there were sixteen different pens to choose from, only 30 percent of subjects bought one. And it's not just pens: psychologists Sheena Iyengar and Mark Lepper have shown that the same principle applies to Godiva chocolate and fruit jams, as giving people more choice often leads to fewer purchases.[7] Another study by Iyengar and colleagues showed that giving people a large choice set of mutual funds lowered participation rates in 401(k) plans: for every ten additional mutual funds, the participation rate dropped by about 2 percent.[8] Most recently, a study of online wine shoppers found that offering customers fewer options—the scientists removed the lowest-selling wines from consideration—increased consumer satisfaction, at least if the shoppers weren't wine experts.[9]

I think it's fair to say that the online world hasn't grappled with these findings. If anything, it's making the problem worse, strengthening the impact of choice overload. Amazon, for instance, offers consumers 1,047 black roller-ball pens and roughly 1,600 fruit jams. Scottrade, a leading online broker, lets investors pick from thousands of different mutual funds. On site after site, users are inundated with alternatives, their screens filled with possibility. The end result is a mismatch between the amount of available choice and our ability to choose. When this mismatch isn't managed—when the growth of choice is not accompanied by effective choice architectures—consumers tend to disappear.

And it's not just the size of choice sets that can be overwhelming. Too many sites also suffer from a kind of "navigation overload," in which online visitors are besieged by a vast assortment of menu bars, buttons, pop-up windows, and search tools. As a result, it's unclear how they can find what they're looking for, even if they know what they want. Such navigation overload is taxing and tiring; the brain doesn't like feeling lost. Try this exercise at home: Time how long it takes you to count from one to ten. Now time how long it takes you to count from ten down to one. If you're anything like me, it took you far longer to count backward. (My exact numbers are 2.16 seconds going forward and 3.13 seconds going backward.) This is a simple illustration of how we prefer familiar routes and easy-to-navigate paths, whether it's counting in our heads or clicking on a screen. When a Web site presents us with too many unclear routes, it's the design equivalent of forcing people to count backward.

Here's what happens to Web sites that *don't* help people choose online: their audience disappears. PriceGrabber.com is a cautionary tale. Founded in 1999, PriceGrabber was one of the first price-comparison shopping Web sites, allowing consumers to compare prices all across the Internet. Its early entry allowed it to quickly become a popular portal, attracting millions of visitors looking for product information. The path to continued growth seemed obvious: PriceGrabber needed to expand its selection, to crawl the Web for even more alternatives. As such, the growth of its inventory mirrored the growth of the Internet as a whole. Ten years ago, PriceGrabber featured a million different items, from plasma televisions to Legos. But now? They offer *150 million distinct products*. If you include all the different options on those products, such as color and size, then PriceGrabber and its affiliates offer more things for purchase than there are people on the planet. To help people find the right item, it also features a wide variety of navigation tools, including dozens of menu buttons on the home screen and multiple search boxes.

But offering choice by itself is not enough. PriceGrabber learned this the hard way. Although the site is still very successful behind the scenes—PriceGrabber now provides data to many of the major price comparison sites, such as AOL, Microsoft/Bing, and Yahoo!— it is no longer a key destination for consumers. "The consumer side of the business really went away," said Tom MacNeil, the vice president of technology at PriceGrabber. "We're like Myspace. We were big and now we're not . . . And once users leave, it's really hard to get them back."[10]

What happened? Why did PriceGrabber lose market share even as it kept on adding millions of new items? The answer is rooted in that upside-down U-curve. PriceGrabber was so focused on increasing its digital inventory—they wanted to feature every single product for sale on the Internet—that it neglected an even more important part of the online decision-making process, which is helping people figure out what they should choose. They didn't manage the mismatch between the quantity of options and our capacity to find what we want.

The lesson, then, is simple: It's not enough to offer people lots of possibilities on their screens. If you want to succeed, you need to help them find the right one. It doesn't matter if you're offering 150 million products or dozens of different health care plans—customers want Web sites and apps that make it easier for them to make a smart choice.

This chapter is about how to do that.

THE CATEGORY FIX

In the late 1960s, psychologists made a startling discovery about shoppers.[11] While traditional models of choice assumed that consumers contemplated all of the relevant options—that's how we maximized utility—people in the real world turned out to be far less thorough. Instead of thinking about every possibility on the shelf, they very quickly narrowed down the list of items they were going to consider, often by using brands and labels as mental shortcuts. The resulting list was known as a consideration set. What was most noteworthy about such sets is their size, as they typically consisted of fewer than five options. Although there might be thirty-plus deodorants in the average supermarket, the average consumer considers only three brands; the typical drugstore offers more than fifty different shampoos, but shoppers seriously think about buying only four of them. The same ratio applies to most consumer goods, from coffee to cars, as the vast majority of consumers ignore most of what's on the shelf.

Consideration sets were first discovered among shoppers in physical stores, but I think the idea is even more relevant in the digital space. For one thing, consideration sets are a reminder that consumers naturally try to limit their options, especially in a world of abundant choice. As John Hauser, a professor of marketing at MIT, points out, consideration sets are a rational response to a world with too many alternatives and too little time. We don't want to spend hours picking out a shampoo—we just want clean hair.[12]

But the importance of consideration sets also clarifies the challenge for online choice architects. Their goal should be to help consumers narrow down the vast amount of choice on the screen to the best possible consideration set, which contains the items that will make the buyer most satisfied. If people are able to consider only a few options at a time—and not the dozens of options on the screen, or the thousands of options in the warehouse—then we have to make sure they are considering the right ones.

How to do this? One approach involves the introduction of categories, which allow people to eliminate huge swaths of possibility with minimum effort. Given the abundance of the Web, it's not feasible to reject options one at a time—if I spent five seconds contemplating every running shoe on Zappos, it would take me almost an entire day to get through them all. The purpose of a smart category, then, is to ensure that our limited attention is focused on the options we're most interested in.

Look, for instance, at a study published in 2008 by Cassie

Mogilner, Tamar Rudnick, and Sheena Iyengar.[13] In one experiment, the scientists sorted fifty different coffee flavors into ten discrete groupings, such as "spicy" or "mild." After choosing a coffee, and then tasting it, the subjects were asked to rate, on a scale from 1 to 7, how happy they were with their selection. People in the no-category condition gave the coffee an average rating of 3.5, while those allowed to choose among the coffee categories gave their selection a rating of 4.5. (The effect was not significant among coffee aficionados, who already knew exactly what they wanted.) This increase in satisfaction came despite the fact that every subject was given the exact same coffee to taste. According to the scientists, categorization works because it "increases perceptions of variety," which makes consumers more determined to find the best alternative. Instead of getting frustrated by all the irrelevant options, they're able to efficiently zero in on the ideal consideration set.

But categorization by itself is not enough—we must carve up the world into the *right* categories, at least if we want to help people make better decisions. Take a new study of menu categories and consideration sets led by Jeffrey Parker at Georgia State University.[14] In recent years, there has been a dramatic increase in the number of restaurant and fast-food menus featuring a "low-calorie" category of dishes, designed to appeal to the health conscious. However, in a series of experiments, Parker demonstrates that such categories actually make people *less* likely to choose the healthiest dishes. (This effect exists only when the low-calorie options are grouped together, which suggests that the problem isn't the dishes themselves—it's the design of the menu.) The explanation returns us to consideration sets, as Parker hypothesizes that many customers eliminate the entire "low-calorie" category at a glance. We assume these dishes won't be tasty, or will leave us hungry, and so we don't even give them a second thought. This doesn't mean restaurants should eliminate low-calorie options, or not list calorie counts on their menus. But it does suggest that we need to take categories very seriously, for using the wrong category might be worse than using none at all.

Of course, categories in the physical world come with an obvious constraint: they can't be customized. Restaurants typically offer the same menu to everyone, regardless of their personal preferences; stores can't redesign the shelf for different shoppers. The digital space, however, doesn't have these limitations. There is no reason every customer should be shown the same options categorized in the same fashion, for the screen can be carved up in countless ways. In short, online stores can offer us far more variety, but they can also offer us far more *categories*, and these categories can be highly personalized.

Let's see how this might work on Amazon. Right now, Amazon offers more than eight thousand different coffee beans, from more than one hundred different brands. To sort through all these options, Amazon gives users a few broad categories. For instance, I can sort by brand, such as Starbucks (95 options) or Philz (25 options). Or I can filter the beans by suggested keyword, such as espresso (729 options) or kosher (225 options). These categories are certainly helpful, but they still generate extremely large choice sets. Unless I know exactly what I'm looking for—say, a Starbucks espresso blend—then I'm going to end up staring at a screen cluttered with alternatives.

But now imagine that Amazon takes full advantage of the categorization effect. Instead of scrolling through the endless list—depending on my display options, I could be faced with up to four hundred additional pages of options—I would first select from a few categories automatically generated based on my past purchase and search history. (Amazon is already using this information to constantly recommend new products.) Perhaps shoppers like me tend to buy fair trade beans, or prefer coffee with chocolate notes; the data will reveal the relevant correlations. According to the latest research,[15] this strategy would accomplish two objectives: consumers would become more aware of the variety on display and they would be more satisfied with their purchase. They might even discover a new brand that belongs in their consideration set. In this sense, categorization is just a simplified form of search, a means of ensuring that the results are as relevant as possible.

This ability to discover new brands—to delight in the *un*familiar—is actually a crucial test of online choice architecture. Itamar Simonson, a professor of marketing at Stanford, has argued that brands will become far less important in the digital world, as consumers now have access to a wealth of useful, independent information. "Brands are less needed when consumers can assess product quality using better sources of information such as reviews from other users, expert opinion, or information from people they know on social media," he writes.[16] It's an interesting hypothesis, but I'm not entirely convinced. Consider the music industry, which is an example of a domain where the opposite seems to be occurring. Because the online space is so saturated with options—Spotify offers users more than twenty million tracks—people are *more* likely to gravitate toward whatever they recognize. For instance, musical superstars—the top 1 percent of artists—account for 77 percent of all digital revenue from recorded music. That's a 6-percentage-point increase over their share of musical revenue in 2000, when almost all music sales were done in physical stores with limited shelf space.[17] This suggests that in a world of nearly infinite choices and information people are forced to rely on mental shortcuts to carve out their consideration set. These shortcuts aren't necessarily effective—as Simonson points out, they're largely influenced by advertising—but what's the alternative? In a world of scarce attention and excess information, it's too hard to find something better.

However, if a Web site has an effective choice architecture, and takes advantage of categorization, then I think Simonson's theory might hold, as consumers will be exposed to possibilities they never would have considered before. Perhaps it's a new band that plays my favorite category of music, or maybe it's a coffee that fits my category profile: the Web site is acting like the best kind of salesperson, showing me new options that I probably wouldn't have discovered on my own. Instead of being swamped with alternatives, and going with whatever I recognize, I'm able to take advantage of all the variety on display. This suggests that, as Web sites get better at helping us cope with excessive choice, brands might finally become less important, just as Simonson predicts. We don't want endless possibility. What we really crave is effective curation.

If you're familiar with Web design, then there's an obvious objection to these suggestions. It's known as the Three-Click Rule and is frequently taken as gospel, at least among some Web designers. The rule itself is simple to explain: users are supposed to flee Web sites that require them to make more than three clicks in order to complete a task. While the rule was first formulated back in the era of dial-up modems and patchy mobile coverage—a time when Web pages took forever to load, if they loaded at all—the rule is still widely followed. If true, the Three-Click Rule would be a powerful criticism of any choice architecture that employed categories, as each category selection would constitute a click. By the time I narrowed down my coffee options to a manageable consideration set—say, by clicking the most appealing categories—my clicks would be all used up. I wouldn't have any attention left over to pick a coffee. I'm guessing that the Three-Click Rule is one of the reasons Amazon continues to offer consumers as many options as possible on the first search screen. This, after all, is the company that patented the enormously successful "One Click" buying button—they clearly care about minimizing your clicks.

But is there any evidence that the Three-Click Rule is true? Not so much. In a study published by User Interface Engineering, Joshua Porter showed that the number of clicks isn't correlated with completion of a task on a Web site.[18] In fact, he found that many users were willing to make up to twenty-five clicks if they felt like the clicks were helping them get closer to what they were looking for. As Porter notes, one of the most common consumer complaints is how long it takes to find an item. "However, these complaints aren't actually about the clicks," he writes. "They are really complaints about failing to find something. When users find what they want they don't complain about the number of clicks."

The goal, then, shouldn't be the elimination of clicks. Instead, Web sites should strive to make every click useful. (I might rephrase the rule as the "three useless clicks" corollary, since useless clicks clearly drive away customers.) As the research demonstrates, clicking on categories can help us break down an excess of options into a manageable consideration set, filled with relevant options. Instead of relying on brands and logos—traditional consideration sets are strongly influenced by advertising—we can find the products that best fit our desires.

But there's a catch. The category fix works great when it can narrow down the final consideration set to a manageable size, such as three or four items. But what if, even after clicking on all the relevant categories, we still end up with thirty coffee bean alternatives? Or twenty health plans? In these cases, the final consideration set is still way too big; we will be overwhelmed by all the possibilities.

To fix this problem (which is the problem faced by many online retailers) we need to experiment with a far more novel solution, which is possible only in a world of screens. That's where we turn next.

THE TOURNAMENT FIX

The first Wimbledon tennis tournament took place in 1877.[19] There were twenty-two men competing and a few hundred people watching from the stands. (Tickets cost a shilling.) The tournament began with eleven different matches; the British players were randomly pitted against each other. The winners of those matches then moved on to the next round, where they competed against another winner. (To compensate for the odd number of matches, the players drew lots to determine who would be granted a bye to the next round.) This process proceeded for four rounds until a single player remained. His name was Spencer Gore, a surveyor from Wandsworth. His prize was twelve guineas and a silver challenge cup.

While much has changed at Wimbledon over the last 138 years— the winner now receives about $3 million and some tickets cost thousands of dollars—the structure of the tournament has stayed the same. Players must still win or go home; each round eliminates half of the competitors. Because the tournament begins with 128 players, it takes seven rounds before a winner is crowned.[20]

And it's not just Wimbledon: such tournaments have come to

define countless sporting events, from tennis to college basketball. They are called "sequential elimination tournaments." The name is literal: they are an ideal mechanism for eliminating competitors, whittling down a large group of entrants to a single winner.

But here's the surprising part: this same tournament model might also represent an effective solution for dealing with the problem of excessive choice. That, at least, is the provocative idea put forth by Tibor Besedes, an economist at the Georgia Institute of Technology.[21] While most Web sites attempt to display as many options as possible, Besedes wondered if the competing alternatives should be divided into discrete rounds, much like Wimbledon or March Madness. After people select an option from each of these rounds, they would be asked to choose among their previous favorites. In this sense, their final choice is the "winner" of the tournament. Furthermore, because each round consists of a manageable consideration set, people might actually be able to identify the one they want.

It's a clever idea, but does it work? To test his hypothesis, Besedes and colleagues offered people a selection of sixteen decks of cards. Each of the decks had a complex set of outcomes, but one of the decks was objectively ideal—it had the best odds of winning, at least if you were able to decipher the statistical details. As expected, people asked to choose among all sixteen decks at the same time performed the worst. In fact, they selected the optimal deck only 23 percent of the time. Besedes cites this as a clear example of choice overload, as people were unable to handle the surplus of available information.

Now comes the tournament condition. In this shopper's version of Wimbledon, there were four rounds, each of which consisted of four new options. After seeing all of the options, people then made their final selection from the four previously selected decks. When the choices were presented like this, subjects were able to successfully locate the ideal deck 48 percent of the time. In other words, they were more than *twice* as likely to identify the best option. That's a huge increase.

Why was the tournament model so effective? When all of the decks were presented at once, people were held back by the processing bottlenecks of the mind, which can handle only a few pieces of information at any given moment. As a result, the numbers remained indecipherable. However, when these same alternatives were presented in discrete rounds, subjects were better able to sort through all of the probabilities and identify the best decks. "I wanted to find a choice process that didn't take away any options, but also helped people find the most optimal outcome," Besedes says. "And that's what tournaments allow."[22]

There are many obvious applications for this choice architecture. Perhaps the most effective setup involves a combination of sequential tournaments with categorization. Imagine a person looking to rent a New York City apartment. Until a few years ago, this decision typically required the help of a real estate broker, who would listen to your requirements and then take you on a tour of several properties. (Such personalized service didn't come cheap: if an apartment was found, the broker would typically charge 8 to 15 percent of the first year's rent.) The Internet, of course, has completely transformed the selection process, as the vast majority of New York City apartments are now listed online, collected by sites such as Zillow, Craigslist, and Apartable. What's interesting, however, is that brokers still dominate the marketplace, especially for higher-end listings. Unless you get lucky, and happen to stumble upon a gem on Craigslist, you'll probably end up paying more than a month's rent for the privilege of signing a lease.

Why do brokers still play such a big role in the NYC apartment market? Why hasn't the Internet disrupted their business model? While brokers are retained by landlords, and landlords benefit from the low supply of and high demand for NYC apartments, brokers also maintain their hold on the market because it's incredibly difficult to choose an apartment online, even when all the relevant information is present. (This is why the New York City government, on its Web site, advises people to choose a neighborhood and then "find a broker based there.")[23] For instance, when I search for apartments in Greenwich Village on Apartable.com—that's a relatively small Manhattan neighborhood, encompassing about a quarter of a square mile—I come up with more than five thousand options. To make sense of these alternatives, Apartable.com and its competitors let me filter the results. I can sort by price, move-in date, and number of bedrooms. Unfortunately, the choice set is so large that none of these filters makes much of a dent. (Even if I restrict my search to three-bedroom apartments available in the next month, I still end up with nearly five hundred listings.) And so I'm forced to scroll through page after page of pictures and listings, trying to figure out which places are worthy of a visit. Given the huge choice set and ineffective choice architecture, it shouldn't be too surprising that so many people are still forced to rely on a human broker for help and guidance.

But now imagine this decision with personalized categories followed by a choice tournament. First, the users would be asked to select their apartment preferences. What's their ideal location? Do they want a dishwasher? Air-conditioning? (This information is already online; it just hasn't become part of the choice architecture.) If it were up to me, I'd filter the options based on their proximity to my favorite café; someone else might prioritize proximity to a subway station, or care most about square footage. Either way, the purpose of this exercise is to eliminate most of the options before we really start considering them, just like a helpful broker. Then, once we've narrowed down our list to approximately sixteen possibilities, we would be launched into a choice tournament. Four options would appear on the screen, complete with all of their relevant information, such as size, price, and photographs. The customer would make his or her selection, at which point another four options would appear. The process would repeat until all of the relevant apartments had been displayed. Then, the user would enter the final round of the choice tournament, asked to choose among their favorite listings from the earlier rounds. "This is the hard part," Besedes says, "because you're asking the subject to choose among options they've already liked." As a result, they are forced to grapple with the basic trade-offs of real estate and to weigh the relative importance of the different variables. Such a reckoning is never fun, but it's also the essence of good decision making. Besedes's research suggests that if apartment Web sites used this choice architecture, consumers would be much more likely to find the best place given their needs. They might even stop requiring the services of a broker.

But it's important to note that choice tournaments won't solve all of the problems associated with an excessive amount of choice. As numerous studies have pointed out, more options typically lead to less overall satisfaction, even if we've chosen well. Earlier in the chapter, we learned about research conducted by Sheena Iyengar and Mark Lepper, which showed that students given six chocolates to choose from were happier with their choices than students offered thirty different flavors.[24] They thought their chocolates were much tastier. They were also four times as likely to choose a box of chocolates instead of cash at the end of the experiment.

Why did more options make the students less pleased with their choices? Iyengar and Lepper emphasize the importance of buyer's remorse, as the additional chocolates on display caused subjects to question their original decision. They might select the Grand Marnier truffle, but then wonder about the cappuccino bonbon. And so they kept thinking about the chocolates, wondering if there was a better one.

This is known as postchoice regret, and it's a serious problem in a world of countless alternatives and endless information. But it turns out that this problem comes with a simple solution, which is perfectly suited for screens.

THE CLOSURE FIX

There's a revealing scene in the 2009 movie *It's Complicated*. The plot is the usual melodrama: Jane, played by Meryl Streep, has started sleeping again with her ex-husband, Jake (Alec Baldwin). But she's also begun a relationship with Adam (Steve Martin), the architect redoing her home. The movie is about Jane's paralyzing indecision, as she swings back and forth between the two men. Toward the end of the movie, Jane bakes a chocolate cake for Jake, only to have him not show. Tired of waiting, Jane covers the cake with a lid and goes to bed. Nothing is said, but it's clear what's happened—their relationship is finally over. She is ready to move on.

David Faro, a professor at the London Business School, cites this cinematic moment as an example of what he calls "choice closure," which is the "psychological process by which decision-makers come to perceive a decision to be complete and settled." In a 2013 paper, Yangjie Gu, Simona Botti, and Faro showed how even minor physical acts (such as putting a lid over a cake) can give us a little closure on a difficult choice, and thus prevent a downward spiral of regret.[25]

In one experiment, the scientists asked students to pick a chocolate to eat. Some students were offered twenty-four different options, while others were given only six. After tasting their chocolates, half of the subjects were then told to put a lid over the unchosen chocolates. The scientists hypothesized that this minor act would give them a measure of closure, especially if they were choosing from a large choice set.

That's exactly what happened. In the no-closure condition—these subjects merely tasted their chocolates—larger choice sets led to less satisfaction. However, putting a lid over the chocolates muted the effect. According to Faro, that's because closing the lid after making a choice from a large set minimized thoughts about forgone alternatives and regret. Instead of worrying about all their other candy possibilities, these consumers were able to enjoy the one they'd chosen; the variety had become a benefit instead of a burden. In a follow-up experiment, Faro and colleagues showed that a similar effect occurred when people ordered tea off a menu. Some left the menu open—the no-closure condition—while others were told to snap it shut after making their choice. It turned out that simply closing the menu made people more satisfied with their choices. "What makes this result interesting is that we increased their choice satisfaction without having to give them fewer choices," Faro says. "Instead, we changed the way they felt [about their choice] by manipulating these subtle acts of closure."[26]

In a forthcoming paper, Faro and colleagues show that a similar sense of closure can also be triggered by simple visual cues on screens, such as stamping forgone alternatives "REJECTED," or drawing a line between the chosen item and all the other unchosen options.[27] "I think this has direct application to the digital world," Faro told me. "It's not just physical acts, like closing a menu, that give you closure. You can get the same thing with visuals on a screen." But you do have to get the visuals right, and make it easier for people to let go of what they did not choose.

Alas, many Web sites get this process exactly backward. Rather than encourage closure, they actively undermine it. For instance, after I add an item to my shopping cart at Amazon, the site sends me to a screen filled with similar products. Some of these products are complementary—after I choose a coffee bean, they might show me a selection of coffee makers. However, one section of the screen is particularly problematic, as it features *competing* products. (It's the "Customers who bought this item also bought" feature.) Although I've just made a difficult decision, winnowing down a huge choice set to a single alternative, Amazon seems determined to prevent any sense of closure. This might occasionally result in additional sales— I'm sure Amazon knows exactly how effective it is—but the sales pitch might also come with a hard-to-measure cost, as it probably undermines my future satisfaction.

ONLINE CHOICE ARCHITECTURE

It's time to put all these fixes together, to explore how this new research can reshape the way we choose on screens, especially in an age of intimidating abundance, when there are more options than we could possibly consider. We might be more overwhelmed than ever before, but at least we have the means of dealing with our bounded brain.

My case study will be healthcare.gov, because I believe that improving the design of this site could have significant societal benefits for three reasons. First, there are still tens of millions of people living without health insurance. Because most of the uninsured have few assets, they are at high risk of being driven into poverty or bankruptcy by unexpected health care costs. While a good Web site won't solve this problem, it will almost certainly help, as it will make it easier for people to purchase the best plan for them and their families. (Remember that one of the main reasons people didn't sign up for a Medicare Part D plan is because the process was too complicated.) The second reason is that, even for those who do have health insurance, it remains a major expense—in 2013, the average household spent $3,631 on health care; among families with kids, or people without employer-subsidized insurance, the costs are far higher.[28] Last, I want to focus on healthcare.gov because research suggests that a lot of people choose badly and pick the wrong plans. In a recent paper, Saurabh Bhargava, George Loewenstein, and Justin Sydnor analyzed the health insurance choices of fifty-five thousand employees at a Fortune 100 company.[29] They discovered that the vast majority of workers made poor insurance decisions, which cost them, on average, about 2 percent of the typical employee's salary. (Among women and workers with lower income, these poor decisions wiped out 4 to 5 percent of their annual salary, or half a month of work.) These are not trivial mistakes. These choices have consequences.

Why do we get it so wrong? The first thing to note is that health insurance is really complicated—it's a decision filled with difficult trade-offs and unfamiliar jargon. (In a survey conducted by Loewenstein and several colleagues, only 14 percent of subjects understood the basic concepts of the insurance marketplace, such as co-pay and coinsurance.)[30] The challenging nature of this decision leads many people to make mistakes. To help you understand one common mistake, I'm going to offer you two health insurance plans. These plans are identical beyond the differences in the monthly premium and the deductible, which includes your out-of-pocket expenses. Please pick the one you'd prefer:

Plan A has a monthly premium of $150 and a deductible of $1,000

Plan B has a monthly premium of $100 and a deductible of $1,500

If you're like most people, you picked Plan A.[31] It probably seemed like the more responsible and less risky option, since it came with a deductible that was 33 percent lower. However, choosing a low-deductible plan is often the incorrect choice, since low deductibles require higher monthly premiums. If you *never* got sick, for instance, then Plan B is obviously the better choice, since you wouldn't have to worry about your higher deductible. (You'd pay only $1,200 in premiums.) However, even if you did get sick and used up your *entire* deductible, Plan B is still the best choice. After all, the maximum annual cost of Plan A is $2,800 ($1,800 in annual premiums, plus a $1,000 deductible). That's still $100 more than the worst-case scenario of Plan B, which is $2,700 ($1,200 in premiums, plus a $1,500 deductible). This means that, no matter what happens to you, the lower-premium plan is a smarter option.

Unfortunately, consumers shopping for insurance are often excessively risk averse, and tend to go with higher premium/lower deductible plans. For instance, in that study of workers at the Fortune 100 firm, 65 percent of subjects chose more expensive plans with lower deductibles, even though a few seconds of arithmetic could have revealed their poor choice. And this isn't an isolated example. According to a study by Jason Abaluck and Jonathan Gruber at MIT, senior citizens signing up for Medicare Part D spent significantly more money than they needed to simply because they opted for plans with low deductibles.[32] The same pattern applies to healthcare.gov, as a typical forty-year-old couple in good health who chose the wrong plan would spend roughly $6,000 more on health insurance for no additional benefits. Again and again, consumers show a strong distaste for out-of-pocket health expenses, at least when compared with spending on insurance premiums. It's a very costly decision-making error, and it's only one of many we make when choosing health insurance.

How can we help people make better choices? It's clear we need a new approach, as many of the strategies we currently use seem to make the problem even worse. A recent study by Peter Ubel, David Comerford, and Eric Johnson showed that healthcare.gov's use of metal labels—each plan was categorized as bronze, silver, gold, or platinum, depending on the percentage of health care costs covered—didn't improve people's insurance choices.[33] The scientists demonstrated this by mischievously switching the labels assigned to the plans in the bronze and gold categories. As Ubel and colleagues note, this switch shouldn't make much of a difference. Instead, consumers should make their choices on the basis of a plan's attributes.

But that's not what the scientists found. After switching the metal labels, they found that people below the median in mathematical ability were far more likely to prefer the gold plans, even when they were actually bronze plans in disguise. Rather than help people focus on the most relevant insurance variables, the metal labels seem to be a distraction.

A similar lesson emerged from research I conducted with Bhargava and Loewenstein. In our experiment, we asked several hundred subjects about their medical history and expected medical usage in the near future. Then we asked them to choose a health insurance plan using the Obamacare choice architecture. We also found that the metal labels failed to help people, with the average subject choosing a plan that was $888 more expensive than it needed to be. (This was equivalent to roughly 3 percent of their income.) In fact, people made worse decisions using the metal labels than they did when the plans were given generic names, such as Plan A and Plan B.

I worry that the surfeit of choice has only exaggerated these decision-making mistakes. Giving us more options doesn't make it easier for us to find the best one—it just makes us more confused, as we get overwhelmed by the information on the screen and rely on misleading mental shortcuts instead. Those employees at the Fortune 100 firm, for instance, were offered forty-eight different health care plans. (A few years before, they'd been offered only three plans: basic, plus, and premium.) But all these new choices didn't improve outcomes, as only about 11 percent of employees were able to find the plan that best fit their needs.

My hope is that this new research on digital decision making can help fix the broken health insurance Web site. At the moment, my proposals are speculative. I'm currently working with Bhargava and

Loewenstein to test some of our hypotheses, but far more research is needed. Nevertheless, I'd like to offer a few possible ideas, if only to get the conversation started.

Let's start with the essential problem faced by healthcare.gov and so many other popular Web sites: choice overload. Imagine you're a single person living in Seminole County, Florida, confronted with 169 health insurance options on healthcare.gov. (The number of plans offered to the average consumer across America was forty-seven.)[34] The plans are listed on the site according to the monthly premium, with each screen offering seven to ten options. This meant that a citizen of Seminole County would have to read (and remember) the plans listed on at least seventeen different screens before making a fully informed choice. Our goal is to reduce this choice set to a manageable consideration set of four. The use of four is deliberate, as a final choice set of three or five would create a bias for the middle option, even if it's not ideal.[35] I'd like to avoid that.

The question, of course, is how we might narrow down the possibilities from 169 to 4. One strategy is to use a variety of tailored, yet easy-to-understand categories. In our online experiments, we found that we could significantly improve health insurance choices— saving people more than $300 on average—by sorting plans according to a subject's expected medical usage. For instance, instead of applying metallic labels to the plans, we referred to them as Low Medical Use, Medium Medical Use, or High Medical Use plans. (A cheap bronze plan is best for someone with expected Low Medical Use.) These new categories don't solve the problem, but they do help people find more suitable insurance options. I believe selection could be improved even further by adding categories that allow consumers to filter options according to their priorities, such as average wait time or the availability of private rooms. (I would try to avoid categories, such as the size of the health network, that lead to higher expenses but have not been shown to improve health outcomes.) The goal is to help consumers quickly, and with only a few clicks, to eliminate the majority of less attractive plans.

After the choice set has been winnowed down with relevant and easy-to-understand categories, I would then launch the user into a choice tournament. The sixteen remaining alternatives would be randomly assigned to one of four different rounds, with people picking their preferred plan in each round. In the final round, they would choose among their four previously selected plans. Because each consideration set is manageable, people should be better able to handle the basic trade-offs. Finally, all of the unchosen plans would be stamped with a big red X, in order to maximize the closure of consumers. It still won't be an easy decision, but at least it won't be overwhelming.

There is one last point worth mentioning. In the digital age, companies and organizations that build ineffective Web sites put themselves at grave risk of being bypassed. I see little reason why someone couldn't put a more effective Web site "facade" over healthcare.gov, implementing many of the strategies outlined in this chapter. Instead of inundating people with inscrutable alternatives, they could create a user-friendly, aesthetically pleasing design that helps people find the best plan. Once a choice has been made, of course, the relevant information would be passed along to the government. But the actual healthcare.gov site would be avoided.

This "digital bypass" approach could be used in countless circumstances, from the financial sector—many sites are now competing to show you your bank account information—to curated shopping sites, which help people deal with the choice overload on Amazon. (I enjoy Canopy.co, for instance.) In the offline world, such competition requires a massive investment, as one would have to buy real estate and build out physical branches and stores. But now? All it takes is a few behavioral insights and a good programmer. If you're not able to help your customers make better decisions, then someone else will.

My goal is that, by applying this new research on categories, tournaments, and closure to current Web sites, we can help people make better choices online. This is especially important when it comes to significant decisions like health insurance, but the same strategies can also be used when shopping online for coffee, or diapers, or whatever else we buy with a click. What I've outlined here is only a first step, of course—I have no doubt we'll come up with better solutions in the future, as we test these proposals and try out new ones. Nevertheless, I think it's time to start taking advantage of all these new digital choice architectures, which allow us to assist with the decision-making process in unprecedented ways. We can choose to choose better.

ASK YOURSELF

In the digital age, we have more choice than ever before. We might also be choosing worse than ever before. For this chapter, I've structured my questions as a "choice algorithm." The goal of the algorithm is to take a huge choice set—say, 4^5, or 1,024, options—down to an ideal consideration set of 4^1, or 4.

1. Your online shelf might have thousands of options, but have you given consumers the tools to find a suitable consideration set of, say, four alternatives? (Mathematically, think of this as reducing a set from 4^{MANY} to 4^1.)

2. Have you considered the "easy-middle bias" when setting the size of the consideration set? A consideration set of three or five options might steer people toward the middle option, whereas a consideration set of four options will likely trigger more thinking about trade-offs.

3. One useful approach to getting to a manageable consideration set involves the use of categories. Have you tried personalized categories? The digital environment offers many more ways to slice the shelf, which could be tailored to each individual.

4. Are you too worried about the number of clicks required during the decision-making process? While fewer clicks is

preferable, the more critical insight is to make the clicks useful.

5. Have you considered choice tournaments to reduce the options from sixteen to four? Such tournaments can be especially helpful if the alternatives involve several different variables and trade-offs. (Mathematically, think of this as reducing a set of 4^2 to 4^1.)

6. Are you managing regret? Research shows that marking unattractive options "DECLINED" can enhance choice closure. It's a very low-cost way to increase consumer satisfaction.

7. Are you also considering attribute overload? Cognitive overload isn't caused only by the number of options—it can also be triggered by the number and complexity of attributes. Displaying dozens of features of each health care plan, for instance, could result in confused users, even if the consideration set is just three or four options.

8. Are you trusting my advice too much? While there is a lot of research to back up my recommendations, it is equally important to test the actual user experience and choice quality and adjust the design accordingly.

CHAPTER 8

Thinking Architecture

One of my main goals in this book has been to show how the digital world might benefit from the insights of behavioral science. In part, this is because behavioral science is able to study the digital mind, and thus predict how we'll react to particular screen environments. We can anticipate what **Comic Sans** does to our reading comprehension, and make educated guesses about the impact of placing an item in the center of the screen.

The digital world needs these insights, at least when it comes to helping people make decisions in their long-term interests. Although our screens are pretty good at distracting us with ads and click-bait headlines, they're less effective at getting us to remember what we read, or find the best insurance plan. Consider the abundance of health apps for mobile devices: in Apple's app store, there are currently more than forty-three thousand different options. Alas, almost all of these programs are useless. A recent analysis concluded that more than 90 percent of health apps provided little to no medical value. Both consumers and businesses are wasting their money on digital "fixes" that fix nothing.[1]

How can we use behavioral science to improve this situation? So far, this book has focused on two tools of behavioral science: *information architecture* and *choice architecture*. Information architecture refers to the ways in which the format of information can change the way we process it—the use of disfluent fonts, for instance, can lead to better digital reading comprehension—while choice architecture shows how the design and layout of alternatives on screens can impact our decisions. (Choice tournaments are a clear example of a new kind of choice architecture, which is far easier to employ online.) To give you a sense of how these tools can be used in the digital world, let's see how they might help us solve a serious societal problem.

The problem I'd like to focus on is the retirement savings crisis. Roughly two thirds of Americans say they aren't saving enough.[2] Meanwhile, a study by Alicia Munnell, the director of the Center for Retirement Research at Boston College, finds that about half (52 percent) of all households are at risk of not maintaining their quality of life in retirement.[3] That's an increase of more than 20 percentage points since the 1980s.

So how can the behavioral science of screens help? Here's one proposal: we should create a retirement savings app for our smartphones that both increases our motivation to save and makes saving as easy as possible. Let's begin with information architecture. One of the big problems with the retirement savings crisis is that most people fail to empathize with the needs of their future self. As a result, we overemphasize the needs of our present self, indulging in all sorts of immediate gratifications. In chapter 6, we looked at the benefits of personalized self-portraits, and how digitally aging a picture of someone so they look much older can increase their motivation to save for retirement. (Because the picture makes our older self more tangible—it closes the so-called empathy gap—people are less likely to discount the future.) In our savings app, people would be shown these digitally altered portraits before making major savings decisions.

But it's not enough to just make people more aware of their need to save—we also need to make it easier for them to act on the information. And that takes us to choice architecture: we should make it as effortless as possible for people to make the right decision, by stripping away all the struggle and frustration that keep them from doing the responsible thing. That, at least, is the primary lesson of Save More Tomorrow, the plan I developed with Richard Thaler that has increased the savings rates of millions of Americans. Because we made the act of increasing their savings rates mostly painless— we asked them to commit to saving more every time they got a pay raise—people were far more likely to do it. And then, once they committed to future saving increases, the "autopilot" feature of the program made it easy to save a lot more.

I'd like to extend this logic to the digital world. Because the phone company already knows your name, birth date, Social Security number, and address, the app could automatically fill out the required financial forms; it shouldn't take more than one click to register.[4] After an account is established, consumers could automatically send the desired amount to their retirement savings account every month. (The charges would later appear on their phone bill. Alternatively, one could link up a debit card directly.) For the first time ever, it will be as easy to save money as it is to spend money.

Of course, these digital fixes won't solve the savings crisis. But I believe they could put a significant dent in the problem, just like Save More Tomorrow did. What's more, by encouraging researchers to experiment with digital nudges, this app would help us figure out what sort of information and choice architectures are most effective. Do people save more for retirement when they get a free iTunes download with every deposit? What time of day is best when making such appeals? Will people save more if they know how much their peers are saving? If we can fine-tune our nudges, then I think we could begin to solve one of the most pressing questions in the social sciences: how to get people to plan more effectively for the future. This is crucial for retirement savings, of course, but also for issues like the obesity epidemic, global warming, and even the national debt. Time and time again, we overvalue today at the expense of tomorrow. I want to help people focus more on tomorrow, and I think our digital devices can help.

However, if we're really serious about tackling the retirement savings crisis, then we need to take advantage of another behavioral tool. John Payne and I call it *thinking architecture*, and I believe it's a strategy that can best be utilized in the digital space. If information architecture makes us more aware of the most relevant information, and choice architecture makes it easier for us to make better choices, then thinking architecture is about helping us think smarter.

Here's how thinking architecture could be used to help people save more money for the future. My approach involves something called "query theory." First developed by the psychologists Eric Johnson, Gerald Häubl, and Anat Keinan, query theory is premised on the belief that, when people make a decision, they often arrive at their decision by asking themselves a series of internally posed questions. In a variety of experiments, Johnson and colleagues have shown that query theory can help explain many long-standing quirks of human behavior, from the endowment effect[5]—a tendency to overvalue those things we own—to inconsistencies in political beliefs.[6]

The influence of these questions has also been documented in a recent randomized controlled trial (RCT) led by the Behavioural Insights Team in the British government. The goal of the study was to increase the number of organ donors, and thus hopefully relieve the severe shortage of available organs for transplant. In Britain, people are typically asked to become donors after registering online for a driver's license or when renewing their vehicle tax. To help boost the donor rate, the Behavioural Insights Team tested eight different short messages, each of which was randomly shown to more than 135,000 people.[7] While most of the variants led to a slight increase in the percentage of people choosing to become donors, at least when compared with a control condition, one variant was clearly the most effective. The message was short and sweet, and stressed the element of reciprocity: "If you needed an organ transplant would you have one? If so please help others." When people were asked that question before making an organ donor decision, they were nearly a third more likely to sign up and become donors. If it is implemented online, the Behavioural Insights Team estimates that this minor design change would lead to 96,000 additional organ donors. Lives will be saved, all because they found the right question to ask on a screen.

I believe a similar strategy could also be used to encourage people to make more prudent financial decisions. In a 2007 paper, a team of psychologists showed that by simply changing the sequence of questions—having people think first about why it would be good to delay gratification, and not indulge—subjects became more likely to wait for a bigger reward.[8] The same approach might also help people save money for retirement. The key is to get people to ask themselves "Why should I save money?" *before* they ask "Why should I *not* save money?" The order of questions is critical.

This could be an important component of the savings app. Let's say, for instance, that your phone knows (thanks to geolocation data) that you're walking in a mall, or driving to Costco. At such moments, it might be helpful to have the gadget prompt you to think of reasons why you might want to save instead of spend. You're still free to treat yourself, obviously; the goal of the app is merely to get you to think, if only for a few moments, about why you might *not* want to.

We're used to checklists for actions, whether it's an airline pilot checking his cockpit controls or a surgeon following surgical protocol. At its core, thinking architecture is a checklist for our thoughts. Such checklists are often a little tedious, but here's the thing: *they work*.

THINKING APPS

Thinking architecture is a relatively new, and largely underutilized, approach. However, I believe it has great potential, especially when coupled with these powerful computers we slip into our pockets and purses. In this final section, I'd like to outline three examples of thinking architecture apps that can lead to dramatically improved decisions. I want to make clear that my thinking in this area has been heavily influenced by my friend John Payne, who is a giant in the field.

The first app is for football coaches. A few years ago, the economist David Romer published a paper examining the fourth-down decisions of coaches in the NFL.[9] For those who don't follow football—and I'm definitely one of those people—it's enough to know that these decisions are often quite difficult, as the coaches must choose between going for it and kicking the ball, either as a punt or as a field goal. In general, going for it is the riskier alternative, because you have the upside of earning more points, but you also increase the likelihood of getting no points. It's a classic strategic calculation, and the job of a coach is to figure out when taking a risk is worth it.

What made Romer's paper so interesting is that he showed how NFL coaches—professionals paid millions of dollars for their strategic wisdom—often make the wrong call, at least according to the statistical odds. Here's an example of a typical fourth-down error. Let's say you're the coach of a team with the ball on the 2-yard line of your opponent. (That means you're only two yards away from a touchdown.) But now it's fourth down—you've got one last play to score. There are two options. As Romer wrote, "Attempting a field goal is virtually certain to produce three points, while trying for a touchdown has about a three-sevenths chance [42 percent] of producing seven points." The two choices thus have the same expected immediate payoff, as three points for sure is equivalent to a three-sevenths chance of getting seven points (3/7 × 7 = 3). It shouldn't be too surprising, then, that the vast majority of coaches in this situation opt for the assured gain of a field goal. As Daniel Kahneman and Amos Tversky demonstrated in the 1970s, people are loss averse: when offered a gamble, we accept the possibility of a loss only if the potential gain is much greater.[10]

As Romer points out, this aversion to potential losses can lead coaches astray. Let's return to our hypothetical fourth-down decision on the 2-yard line. While the expected point payoff is virtually the same, coaches shouldn't just narrowly think about points when making this decision. Instead, they should also consider the broader context of the game, such as field position. For example, if the coach goes for it and fails, then the opponent will take over on their own 2-yard line, leaving them just about as far as possible from the opposing end zone. However, if they kick a field goal, then their opponent will get to return the ensuing kickoff, leaving them significantly closer to a score. This sports decision can be seen as an example of a larger psychological phenomenon: when people think more broadly about the stakes, then risky alternatives might start to feel safer and more attractive.

Unfortunately, most coaches don't engage in broad thinking. Instead, they often rely on a narrow framing of the decision, which leads to some very costly mistakes. In Romer's data set, he found that there were 1,068 fourth downs in which his statistical analysis suggested that teams are better off going for it. Among this sample, the head coach decided to kick it 959 times. That means coaches made the wrong call in these situations about 90 percent of the time.

So how can a fourth-down app help? It turns out to be fairly straightforward to program the expected outcomes of fourth-down decisions at various points on the field. If I were a coach, I'd want an app that could help me do just that, providing me with a fast mathematical analysis before I made up my mind. I might not always follow the app—some coaches might go against the odds for a good reason—but I'd be very interested in what the numbers suggest. I'd want to ensure that I wasn't being excessively loss averse, or falling victim to the mistake of narrow framing. As we saw with the research of Philip Tetlock and colleagues in chapter 4, getting feedback on our predictions can dramatically improve them. If nothing else, the feedback can help us understand why we deviate from the numbers, and if such deviations are a good idea. NFL coaches could use the help: although it's been nine years since Romer published his study, most coaches are still too conservative on fourth down. (In 2006, coaches went for it on 11.21 percent of fourth-down attempts; in 2012, that percentage *declined* to 10.05 percent.)[11] Perhaps the app can help reverse this trend.

I'm guessing you're not an NFL coach. Nevertheless, I think there are some important ways in which thinking apps can help you deal with the same underlying errors that plague their fourth-down decisions. For instance, John Payne and I developed a loss aversion calculator, which you can find at www.digitai.org/#lab. By asking people to evaluate a series of gambles, it's possible to assign them a loss aversion score, which informs them how much more strongly they experience losses than gains. Here's a sample question. Please tell me which gamble you prefer:

GAMBLE A: You have an equal chance of winning $100, breaking even, or losing $100.

GAMBLE B: You have an equal chance of winning $300, breaking even, or losing $200.

Based on your answers to this and other questions, the app can help you understand where you fall on the loss-averse spectrum. Are you excessively scared of losing? Or maybe you're not scared enough? While the idea of loss aversion is not new, we've never before had access to a simple tool that can help us become more aware of our loss-averse tendencies.

Such awareness could come with big benefits. For instance, if you're too loss averse, then maybe you're unwilling to get a necessary medical treatment because there's a very small risk of infection, or perhaps you don't get your child vaccinated because you're scared of the potential side effects. Or maybe you're excessively worried about your possessions, and so you choose to buy a very expensive warranty for your brand-new gadget, even though most experts agree this is a waste of money.

Of course, if you're not loss averse at all, then you might err in the opposite direction, and pursue all sorts of dangerous gambles. Perhaps you buy penny stocks based on suspect tips, or take questionable medical supplements. I don't think the app will suddenly cure people of their most dangerous tendencies, but I do think it might help them understand the underlying cause. And once they understand the cause—it's just a quirk of emotion—they can take steps to deal with its effects.

The app can also document the reliability of our loss-averse instincts. By repeatedly testing ourselves against the app, we can better understand the factors that influence our subjective experience of losses. If your loss aversion score spikes every time the stock market sneezes, then you might want to pick a more conservative portfolio, or avoid checking the market too often. (I also wouldn't want to invest my money in a fund managed by someone with unstable scores.) The end goal is to construct a map of our risk instincts, to better understand the mental factors behind so many of our costly decisions.

Finally, I believe that the loss aversion calculator can help people better understand the tendencies of others. According to research by behavioral scientists David Faro and Yuval Rottenstreich, people make systematic mistakes when it comes to estimating the risk preferences of those they don't know.[12] In general, we tend to assume that strangers are less human than we are, and that their risk preferences are more neutral than our own. So let's say you're a heart surgeon, trying to advise a patient about the risks and benefits of a medical procedure. The science suggests that the surgeon will assume the patient is less sensitive to losses than he or she actually is. This could lead to some serious communication issues. If I were a surgeon, I'd definitely want to know my own loss aversion score, but I'd also want to know the scores of my patients, if only so that I could give them advice more in line with their actual preferences. If their loss aversion score falls on an extreme end of the spectrum, then I'd want to take that into account, too.

The same strategy could be used in countless fields, from financial planning to insurance. Unless we understand how other people think about risk—until we know how sensitive they are to the possibility of a loss—then it's hard to give them good advice.

The last thinking architecture app I've developed is probably the most valuable of all. I decided to develop the app for a straightforward reason: most people don't spend nearly enough time thinking about what they want from life. We fail to do this for two main reasons. The first reason is that we're really busy. We've got jobs, kids, responsibilities. We're often so fixated on getting the little stuff right that it's hard to find time to reflect on the big stuff. The second reason is less flattering: we're cognitively lazy. We don't like to think. And when we do think, we tend to think too quickly and not deeply or broadly enough. (One recent study found that two thirds of male subjects would prefer to give themselves electrical shocks rather than sit alone with their thoughts for fifteen minutes.)[13] Simply put, thinking deeply about difficult issues makes our heads hurt.

However, while technology is part of the problem—it's made it harder than ever to step back and contemplate the big questions—I think it can also be part of the solution. That's why the Allianz Global

Investors Center for Behavioral Finance created an app called the Retirement Goal Planning System (GPS), which you can download for free on Apple's app store. (I am currently the chief behavioral economist of the Allianz Global Investors Center for Behavioral Finance.) In essence, the GPS app tries to lead you through a structured thinking process so that you can think more carefully about what you really want from your life, especially as you near retirement age. (If you'd like to learn about the GPS process, as well as the research behind it, you can read my short book about it that I wrote with Roger Lewin.)[14] For instance, researchers have found that most people aren't very good at coming up with a comprehensive list of life goals by themselves. I might remember that I want to spend more time with my family and travel more often to Israel, but I often forget that I also want to find time for my hobbies, such as composing music. Because we think so infrequently about our major life goals, we aren't very good at planning for them.

The best way to demonstrate this is to give you an exercise. (I promise it's the last one.) On a blank piece of paper, I'd like you to list all of your major goals for retirement. Take as much time as you need. When you're done, put the paper aside.

What I'd like to do now is provide you with a comprehensive "master list" of life goals that you can choose from. This list has been drawn from interviewing dozens of financial advisers and people approaching retirement:

1. Financial Independence: Knowing I can pay my basic expenses for as long as I live
2. Health Care: Being able to pay for my medical expenses
3. Housing: Choosing my own living situation

4. Travel and Leisure: Taking trips and doing fun activities

5. Lifestyle: Maintaining my current lifestyle

6. Second Career: Beginning a new career

7. Self-Improvement: Investing in personal growth

8. Family Bequests: Leaving money to my family

9. Giving Back: Contributing to causes that are important to me

10. Social Engagement: Enjoying the company of friends

11. Ending Life with Dignity: Preparing to experience my last days my way

12. Control: Feeling that I still "drive" my own life

Please select all of the goals in this master list that matter to you. You may select as many or as few goals as are relevant. It's important that you not look back at your original list.

All done? Now please compare your two lists. If you're like most people, then the second list is significantly longer, and includes several important goals not included in the first thought exercise. These additional goals are your life planning blind spots. What's amazing about this exercise is that, even though I warned you that most people struggle to list all of their goals, I'm guessing you suffered from the same blind spot. The rule of thumb is that most people are going to miss half of their goals, and the ones they miss will be just as important as the ones they listed on their own.[15]

It's worth noting, of course, that it didn't take much to reveal your blind spots—all it took was a small amount of thinking architecture and five minutes of your attention. Of course, once you've got a more complete list of life goals, it's important to figure out your priorities, or which goals matter the most. The GPS system does this through a prompted ranking system, in which you are asked to choose your most and least important goals, and then prioritize the remaining ones into three categories. (It's often much easier for people to sort goals into a few buckets, such as "very important" or "somewhat important," rather than having to rank them in a list.) None of this is complicated or tricky or high-tech. In fact, it might even strike you as blindingly obvious. But here's the thing: we never actually do it. And you can't plan for goals you never think about.

My hope is that these simple thinking exercises, which can be done on a touchscreen tablet in a few spare minutes, will help us think more effectively about the future, just as the fourth-down app might help NFL coaches, or the loss aversion app might help investors and doctors making risky decisions. By guiding us through a sequence of choreographed exercises, and by taking our mental blind spots into account, those exercises can help us figure out what we most want from life.

The larger lesson is that we can use these gadgets for much more than shopping and texting and entertainment. There's nothing wrong with those activities, of course—I enjoy them as much as you do. But let's not forget that a powerful assistant and adviser lurks behind those high-resolution screens, and that the devices are capable of improving our own thinking process. We're all familiar with the traditional GPS feature on our phones, which helps us navigate in unfamiliar places. The GPS app is a little different, because it isn't designed to give you the best or quickest route. Rather, it's about helping you figure out your destination, or where you really want to go. Unless you know that, all the technology in the world won't help you get there.

ASK YOURSELF

Our digital devices make it easy to distract ourselves with constant updates; the inbox is never still. But this frenetic pace makes it even more important that we find time to reflect on big, difficult questions.

1. What should you be asking yourself that you are not?

SUMMARY: TOOLS FOR THE FUTURE

This book is about how we think on screens. In part, it is a story of *difference*, a tale of how these screens present us with more information, more choices, and encourage us to act faster than ever before. But I hope the main takeaway has been the tremendous opportunity here, how we can use the insights of behavioral science to design a digital world that helps us think more effectively. Instead of summarizing the entire book, I thought I'd take some of my own advice and try compressing many of the ideas we've discussed into a short list of useful tools for creating smarter screens. Given the scarcity of attention, I've narrowed down my list to what I consider to be the top ten tools for triggering behavioral change on screens. (If you'd like the complete list of forty-two tools mentioned in this book, check out the appendix.)

1. Factor in the attention environment
2. Use information compression techniques
3. Maximize visceral beauty
4. When in doubt, err on the side of simplicity
5. Optimize the use of hotspots
6. Make us *feel* the feedback
7. Use cognitive disfluency to slow the mind down
8. Offer a manageable consideration set

9. Create thinking tools

10. Use science to drive your design and A/B testing

What should we do with all these new tools and insights? My goal is to maximize the upside of the digital world, to take advantage of all these remarkable new tools that exist on screens. Who would have guessed that Photoshopping a selfie to look older would encourage people to save more money, or that a simple thinking app could help people do a much better job of thinking about their life goals? By merging the disciplines of technology and psychology, I believe we can design digital environments that magnify our strengths and let us cope with our weaknesses. Hopefully, the short list above gives you a sense of the possibilities, of all the tools and insights that can be used to influence and improve our online decisions. If nothing else, this research is a reminder that even simple changes to screens can make us smarter and more prudent, better able to focus on what matters.

The progress of technology is swift. Just a few generations ago, people encountered screens only at the movie theater. Then, the screen entered the house, and people spent hours every day staring passively at their televisions. Now we spend a huge chunk of our waking life *interacting* with screens. These screens entertain us and keep us company; they mediate our social interactions and give us feedback on our gym workout; they are where we work and where we relax. This shift toward the digital world represents a remarkable opportunity, a once-in-a-lifetime chance to rethink the possibilities of human behavior. My worry is that we're wasting this moment, chasing clicks instead of changing lives.

We seem to think differently online. I want us to think *better.* If we get the tools right, then I believe we have a chance to improve the choices of everyone staring at a screen.

APPENDIX:
THE COMPLETE LIST OF TOOLS

MENTAL SCREEN

Focus on the mental, not the physical, screen

Factor in the attention environment

Use information compression techniques

Incorporate attention filters

FUNCTION FOLLOWS FORM

"Fast-test" your site

Maximize visceral beauty

When in doubt, err on the side of simplicity

Remember: function follows form

DISPLAY BIASES

Optimize the use of hot spots

Avoid cold spots

Consider cultural differences in hotspot location

Factor in the horizontal bias

Sometimes zoom out, not in

NEW MIRROR

Calibrate the amount of feedback

Use just-in-time education

Leverage the fresh start effect

Make us *feel* the feedback

Use carrots (and not sticks) whenever possible

Be aware of social media conformity effects

Take screen anonymity into account

Empower feedback with an action plan

DESIRABLE DIFFICULTY

Consider ugly fonts (and other forms of visual disfluency)

Use cognitive disfluency to slow the mind down

Calibrate disfluency to fit your site's goals

DIGITAL TAILORING

Use personalized visuals and videos

Tailor the timing of messages

Tailor the menus to each individual

Offer more than one Web site

Remember: too much personalization can backfire

CHOICE OPPORTUNITY

Offer a manageable consideration set

Personalize categories

Incorporate choice tournaments

Manage regret with choice closure

Avoid navigation overload

Manage attribute overload

Maximize satisfaction, not clicks

THINKING APPS

Start with choice architecture

Set the right information environment

Offer thinking tools

GENERAL

Use science to drive your design and A/B testing

Conduct a whiteboard exercise periodically

Remember: the medium shapes the message

NOTES

INTRODUCTION

1. Saurabh Bhargava, George Loewenstein, and Shlomo Benartzi, "The Health Exchanges and the Behavioral Economics of Plan Choice," working paper, Carnegie Mellon University, 2015.

2. Eric Johnson, Ran Hassin, Tom Baker, Allison T. Bajger, and Galen Treur, "Can Consumers Make Affordable Care Affordable? The Value of Choice Architecture," *PLoS ONE* 8.12 (2013): e81521. doi:10.1371/journal.pone.0081521.

3. http://aspe.hhs.gov/health/reports/2014/Premiums/2014MktPlace PremBrf.pdf, p. 10.

4. http://www.nytimes.com/2011/01/17/technology/17brain.html?page wanted=all; http://www.nytimes.com/2010/05/30/world/asia/30drone.html.

5. http://www.nytimes.com/2009/03/17/business/17uav.html?_r=1&hp; see also http://www.nytimes.com/2010/01/11/business/11drone .html?pagewanted=all.

6. Ryan McKendrick, Tyler Shaw, Ewart de Visser, Haneen Sager, Brian Kidwell, and Raja Parasuraman, "Team Performance in Networked Supervisory Control of Unmanned Air Vehicles Effects of Automation, Working Memory, and Communication Content,"

Human Factors: The Journal of the Human Factors and Ergonomics Society (2013): 0018720813496269.

7. Jessie Y. C. Chen and Carla T. Joyner, "Concurrent Performance of Gunners and Robotics Operator Tasks in a Multitasking Environment," *Military Psychology* 21.1 (2009): 98–113.

8. J. Y. C. Chen and P. I. Terrence, "Effects of Tactile Cueing on Concurrent Performance of Military and Robotics Tasks in a Simulated Multitasking Environment," *Ergonomics* 51.8 (2008): 1137–52.

9. http://www.nytimes.com/2011/01/17/technology/17brain.html?page wanted=all.

10. http://www.nytimes.com/2014/01/12/magazine/is-ubers-surge -pricing-an-example-of-high-tech-gouging.html?_r=0.

11. http://instagram.com/p/h93iXKxyPa/.

12. Tibor Besedes, Cary Deck, Sudipta Sarangi, and Mikhael Shor, "Reducing Choice Overload Without Reducing Choices," *Review of Economics and Statistics*, forthcoming.

13. Maya O. Shaton, "The Display of Information and Household Investment Behavior," working paper, University of Chicago, 2014.

14. Connor Diemand-Yauman, Daniel M. Oppenheimer, and Erikka B. Vaughan, "Fortune Favors the **Bold** (*and the Italicized*): Effects of Disfluency on Educational Outcomes," *Cognition* 118.1 (2011): 111–15.

15. Anne Mangen, Bente R. Walgermo, and Kolbjørn Brønnick, "Reading Linear Texts on Paper Versus Computer Screen: Effects on Reading Comprehension," *International Journal of Educational Research* (2013).

16. Richard H. Thaler and Cass R. Sunstein, *Nudge: Improving Decisions About Health, Wealth, and Happiness* (New Haven: Yale University Press, 2008).

17. Shlomo Benartzi and Richard H. Thaler, "Behavioral Economics and the Retirement Savings Crisis," *Science* 339 (March 8, 2013): 1152–53; Richard H. Thaler and Shlomo Benartzi, "Save More Tomorrow™: Using Behavioral Economics to Increase Employee Saving," *Journal of Political Economy* 112.S1 (2004): S164–S187.

18. S. Adam Brasel and James Gips, "Tablets, Touchscreens, and Touchpads: How Varying Touch Interfaces Trigger Psychological Ownership and Endowment," *Journal of Consumer Psychology* 24.2 (2014): 226–33.

19. Anne Mangen, Bente R. Walgermo, and Kolbjørn Brønnick, "Reading Linear Texts on Paper Versus Computer Screen: Effects on Reading Comprehension," *International Journal of Educational Research* (2013).

20. Avi Goldfarb, Ryan McDevitt, Sampsa Samilia, and Brian Silverman, "The Effect of Social Interaction on Economic Transactions: Evidence from Changes in Two Retail Formats," *Management Science* (February 2015).

CHAPTER 1: THE MENTAL SCREEN

1. http://www.washingtonpost.com/blogs/wonkblog/wp/2013/08/30/travel-agents-we-do-exist/.

2. Max Starkov, "End of the OTA Merchant Model—This Time for Real," HeBS Digital; Madigan Pratt, "Breaking the Hotel Addiction to OTAs," Madigan Pratt & Associates.

3. This is based on a Google search done on October 13, 2014. The search was done on a browser clear of all search history and cookies. Your exact number will almost certainly vary according to your own Google activity.

4. http://www.economist.com/node/15557421.

5. http://www-01.ibm.com/software/data/bigdata/what-is-big-data.html.

6. Martin Hilbert, "How Much Information Is There in the 'Information Society'?," *Significance* 9.4 (2012): 8–12.

7. Herbert Simon, "Designing Organizations for an Information-Rich World," in Martin Greenberger, *Computers, Communication, and the Public Interest* (The Johns Hopkins Press, 1971), 37–72.

8. Daniel M. Oppenheimer, Tom Meyvis, and Nicolas Davidenko, "Instructional Manipulation Checks: Detecting Satisficing to Increase Statistical Power," *Journal of Experimental Social Psychology* 45.4 (2009): 867–72.

9. http://www.wordstream.com/articles/google-earnings.

10. http://boardingarea.com/loyaltytraveler/2013/12/05/otas-gain-hotel
    -booking-market-share-in-2013-why/#sthash.HIT2kDcV.dpbs.

11. George Miller, "The Magical Number Seven, Plus or Minus Two,"
    The Psychological Review 63 (1956). See also the version of Miller's
    magical-number paper as delivered at MIT: "Human Memory and
    the Storage of Information," *Institute of Radio Engineers [IEEE]
    Transactions on Information Theory* 2.3 (1956): 129–37.

12. Meredyth Daneman and Patricia A. Carpenter, "Individual Differences
    in Working Memory and Reading," *Journal of Verbal Learning and
    Verbal Behavior* 19.4 (1980): 450–66.

13. Nelson Cowan, Lara D. Nugent, Emily M. Elliott, Igor Ponomarev,
    and J. Scott Saults, "The Role of Attention in the Development
    of Short-Term Memory: Age Differences in the Verbal Span of
    Apprehension," *Child Development* 70.5 (1999): 1082–97.

14. Nelson Cowan, Troy D. Johnson, and J. Scott Saults, "Capacity Limits
    in List Item Recognition: Evidence from Proactive Interference,"
    Memory 13.3–4 (2003): 293–99; Nelson Cowan, "The Magical Mystery
    Four: How Is Working Memory Capacity Limited, and Why?,"
    Current Directions in Psychological Science 19.1 (2010): 51–57.

15. Baba Shiv and Alexander Fedorikhin, "Heart and Mind in Conflict:
    The Interplay of Affect and Cognition in Consumer Decision Making,"
    Journal of Consumer Research 26.3 (1999): 278–92.

16. Anandi Mani, Sendhil Mullainathan, Eldar Shafir, and Jiaying Zhao,
    "Poverty Impedes Cognitive Function," *Science* 341.6149 (2013):
    976–80.

17. Ibid.

18. Ibid.

19. https://institutional.vanguard.com/iam/pdf/HAS14.pdf?cbdForceDomain
    =true (see figures 21, 24, and 29); Brigitte C. Madrian and Dennis F. Shea,
    "The Power of Suggestion: Inertia in 401(k) Participation and Savings
    Behavior," *The Quarterly Journal of Economics* 116.4 (2001): 1149–87.

20. http://www.vanityfair.com/politics/2012/10/michael-lewis-profile
-barack-obama.

21. Daniel Levitan, *The Organized Mind* (New York: Dutton, 2014),
Kindle location: 1896 of 10691.

22. http://www.wsj.com/articles/SB10001424052970204488304574428750
133812262.

23. Ibid.

24. http://www.va.gov/oig/pubs/VAOIG-12-00900-168.pdf; http://www
.va.gov/oig/pubs/VAOIG-14-02603-267.pdf.

25. Hardeep Singh, Christianne Spitzmueller, Nancy J. Petersen, Mona
K. Sawhney, and Dean F. Sittig, "Information Overload and Missed
Test Results in Electronic Health Record–Based Settings," *JAMA
Internal Medicine* 173.8 (2013): 702–4; Hardeep Singh, Eric J.
Thomas, Shrinidi Mani, Dean Sittig, Harvinder Arora, Donna
Espadas, Myrna M. Khan, and Laura A. Petersen, "Timely Follow-up
of Abnormal Diagnostic Imaging Test Results in an Outpatient
Setting: Are Electronic Medical Records Achieving Their Potential?"
Archives of Internal Medicine 169.17 (2009): 1578–86.

26. Hardeep Singh, Lindsey Wilson, Brian Reis, Mona K. Sawhney,
Donna Espadas, and Dean F. Sittig, "Ten Strategies to Improve
Management of Abnormal Test Result Alerts in the Electronic Health
Record," *Journal of Patient Safety* 6.2 (2010): 121.

27. Clement J. McDonald, "Toward Electronic Medical Record Alerts
That Consume Less Physician Time Letters," *JAMA Internal
Medicine* 173.18 (2013): 1755–56.

28. David L.Strayer, Jason M. Watson, and Frank A. Drews, "Cognitive
Distraction While Multitasking in the Automobile," *Psychology of
Learning and Motivation: Advances in Research and Theory* 54 (2011):
29–58.

29. Ibid.

30. Ibid.

31. Milica Milosavljevic Mormann, Vidhya Navalpakkam, Christof Koch, and Antonio Rangel, "Relative Visual Saliency Differences Induce Sizable Bias in Consumer Choice," *Journal of Consumer Psychology* 22.1 (2012): 67–74.

32. Anandi Mani, Sendhil Mullainathan, Eldar Shafir, and Jiaying Zhao, "Poverty Impedes Cognitive Function," *Science* 341.6149 (2013): 976–80.

33. George Miller, "The Magical Number Seven, Plus or Minus Two," *The Psychological Review* 63 (1956).

34. http://www.pwc.com/gx/en/audit-services/capital-market/ publications/assets/document/pwc-global-top-100-march-update.pdf.

35. http://www.latimes.com/local/california/la-me-mhealth-ucla -women-20141205-story.html#page=1.

36. Meera Viswanathan et al., "Interventions to Improve Adherence to Self-Administered Medications for Chronic Diseases in the United States: A Systematic Review," *Annals of Internal Medicine* 157.11 (2012): 785–95; L. Osterberg and T. Blaschke, "Adherence to Medication," *New England Journal of Medicine* 353 (2005): 487–97; J. J. Mahoney et al., "The Unhidden Cost of Noncompliance," *Journal of Managed Care Pharmacy* 14 (2008): S1–S29.

37. Marie T. Brown and Jennifer K. Bussell, "Medication Adherence: WHO Cares?," *Mayo Clinic Proceedings* 86.4 (2011): 304–14.

38. http://www.nhtsa.gov/people/injury/alcohol/impaired_driving_pg2 /us.htm.

39. http://www.cdc.gov/tobacco/data_statistics/fact_sheets/economics/ econ_facts/index.htm.

40. http://www.wired.com/business/2012/04/ff_abtesting.

CHAPTER 2: FUNCTION FOLLOWS FORM

1. Kyung-Ah Kwon et al., "High-Speed Camera Characterization of Voluntary Eye Blinking Kinematics," *Journal of The Royal Society Interface* 10.85 (2013): 2013.0227.

2. Noam Tractinsky, Avivit Cokhavi, and Moti Kirschenbaum, "Using Ratings and Response Latencies to Evaluate the Consistency of Immediate Aesthetic Perceptions of Web Pages," *Third Annual Workshop on HCI Research in MIS*, Washington, DC, 2004.

3. Gitte Lindgaard et al., "Attention Web Designers: You Have 50 Milliseconds to Make a Good First Impression!," *Behaviour & Information Technology* 25.2 (2006): 115–26.

4. Ben Newell and David R. Shanks, "Unconscious Influences on Decision Making: A Critical Review," *Behavioral and Brain Sciences* 37, no. 01 (2014): 1–19.

5. Janine Willis and Alexander Todorov, "First Impressions: Making Up Your Mind After a 100-ms Exposure to a Face," *Psychological Science* 17.7 (2006): 592–98.

6. Jamie Arndt, Jeff Greenberg, Tom Pyszczynski, and Sheldon Solomon, "Subliminal Exposure to Death-Related Stimuli Increases Defense of the Cultural Worldview," *Psychological Science* 8.5 (1997): 379–85; Mark J. Landau, Sheldon Solomon, Jeff Greenberg, Florette Cohen, Tom Pyszczynski, Jamie Arndt, Claude H. Miller, Daniel M. Ogilvie, and Alison Cook, "Deliver Us from Evil: The Effects of Mortality Salience and Reminders of 9/11 on Support for President George W. Bush," *Personality and Social Psychology Bulletin* 30.9 (2004): 1136–50; Andreas Birgegard and Pehr Granqvist, "The Correspondence Between Attachment to Parents and God: Three Experiments Using Subliminal Separation Cues," *Personality and Social Psychology Bulletin* 30.9 (2004): 1122–35.

7. Gráinne M. Fitzsimons, Tanya L. Chartrand, and Gavan J. Fitzsimons, "Automatic Effects of Brand Exposure on Motivated Behavior: How Apple Makes You 'Think Different,'" *Journal of Consumer Research* 35.1 (2008): 21–35.

8. Ap Dijksterhuis, "Think Different: The Merits of Unconscious Thought in Preference Development and Decision Making," *Journal of Personality and Social Psychology* 87.5 (2004): 586.

9. John Payne, in-person interview, February 16, 2015.

10. http://time.com/12933/what-you-think-you-know-about-the-web-is-wrong/.

11. http://www.forbes.com/sites/stevenbertoni/2014/11/04/exclusive-sean-rad-out-as-tinder-ceo-inside-the-crazy-saga/.

12. Aniko Hannak et al., "Measuring Price Discrimination and Steering on E-commerce Web Sites," *Proceedings of the 14th ACM/USENIX Internet Measurement Conference* (2014).

13. Katharina Reinecke, Tom Yeh, Luke Miratrix, Rahmatri Mardiko, Yuechen Zhao, Jenny Liu, and Krzysztof Z. Gajos, "Predicting Users' First Impressions of Website Aesthetics with a Quantification of Perceived Visual Complexity and Colorfulness," in *Proceedings of the SIGCHI Conference on Human Factors in Computing Systems*, 2049–58, ACM, 2013.

14. Naomi Mandel and Eric J. Johnson, "When Web Pages Influence Choice: Effects of Visual Primes on Experts and Novices," *Journal of Consumer Research* 29.2 (2002): 235–45.

15. Katharina Reinecke, telephone interview, January 14, 2014.

16. Katharina Reinecke and Krzysztof Z. Gajos, "Quantifying Visual Preferences Around the World," *Proceedings of the 32nd Annual ACM Conference on Human Factors in Computing Systems* (ACM, 2014).

17. Claudia Townsend and Suzanne B. Shu, "When and How Aesthetics Influences Financial Decisions," *Journal of Consumer Psychology* 20.4 (2010): 452–58.

18. Andreas Sonderegger and Juergen Sauer, "The Influence of Design Aesthetics in Usability Testing: Effects on User Performance and Perceived Usability," *Applied Ergonomics* 41.3 (2010): 403–10.

19. Gitte Lindgaard, Cathy Dudek, Devjani Sen, Livia Sumegi, and Patrick Noonan, "An Exploration of Relations Between Visual Appeal, Trustworthiness and Perceived Usability of Homepages,"

ACM Transactions on Computer-Human Interaction (TOCHI) 18.1 (2011): 1.

20. Lindsay A. Owens, "The Polls—Trends Confidence in Banks, Financial Institutions, and Wall Street, 1971–2011," *Public Opinion Quarterly* 76.1 (2012): 142–62.

21. Ibid.

22. http://www.fdic.gov/householdsurvey/.

23. http://www.consumerfinance.gov/askcfpb/1567/what-payday-loan.html.

24. http://www.fdic.gov/householdsurvey/2012_unbankedreport.pdf, p. 27.

25. http://www.alexa.com/siteinfo/bankofamerica.com, accessed December 24, 2014.

26. I owe a big thank-you to Matt Stewart for helping me implement the algorithm. We tested the Bank of America Web site on July 17, 2014.

27. https://www.javelinstrategy.com/brochure/319; https://smallbusiness .yahoo.com/advisor/marketing-sbos-insights-bank-america-report -220017545.html.

28. http://transition.fcc.gov/Speeches/Tristani/Statements/2001/stgt123.html.

29. http://www.fcc.gov/guides/public-and-broadcasting-july-2008.

30. Linyun W. Yang, Keisha M. Cutright, Tanya L. Chartrand, and Garan J. Fitzsimons, "Distinctively Different: Exposure to Multiple Brands in Low-Elaboration Settings," *Journal of Consumer Research* 40.5 (2014): 973–92.

31. K. E. Stanovich and R. F. West, "Individual Difference in Reasoning: Implications for the Rationality Debate?," *Behavioural and Brain Sciences* 23 (2000): 645–726.

CHAPTER 3: DISPLAY BIASES

1. Ruma Falk, Raphael Falk, and Peter Ayton, "Subjective Patterns of Randomness and Choice: Some Consequences of Collective

Responses," *Journal of Experimental Psychology: Human Perception and Performance* 35.1 (2009): 203.

2. http://search.bwh.harvard.edu/new/presentations/Psychonomics 2012_Drew_Vo.pdf.

3. Nicholas Christenfeld, "Choices from Identical Options," *Psychological Science* 6.1 (1995): 50–55.

4. Elena Reutskaja Rosemarie Nagel, Colin F. Camerer, and Antonio Rangel, "Search Dynamics in Consumer Choice Under Time Pressure: An Eye-Tracking Study," *The American Economic Review* (2011): 900–26.

5. Peter Ayton, telephone interview, July 15, 2014.

6. Milica Milosavljevic Mormann, Vidhya Navalpakkam, Christof Koch, and Antonio Rangel, "Relative Visual Saliency Differences Induce Sizable Bias in Consumer Choice," *Journal of Consumer Psychology* 22.1 (2012): 67–74.

7. Benjamin Libet, Curtis A. Gleason, Elwood W. Wright, and Dennis K. Pearl, "Time of Conscious Intention to Act in Relation to Onset of Cerebral Activity (Readiness-Potential): The Unconscious Initiation of a Freely Voluntary Act," *Brain* 106.3 (1983): 623–42.

8. Mormann, Navalpakkam, Koch, and Rangel, "Relative Visual Saliency Differences Induce Sizable Bias and Consumer Choice," 67–74.

9. Alexander Pollatsek, Jane Ashby, and Charles Clifton Jr., *Psychology of Reading* (New York: Psychology Press, 2012) 385–87.

10. A. Godfroid, "Eye-Tracking," in Peter Robinson, ed., *The Routledge Encyclopedia of Second Language Acquisition* (New York: Routledge, 2013), 234–36.

11. James R. Bettman and Pradeep Kakkar, "Effects of Information Presentation Format on Consumer Information Acquisition Strategies," *Journal of Consumer Research* (1977): 233–40.

12. Savannah Wei Shi, Michel Wedel, and F. G. M. Pieters, "Information Acquisition During Online Decision Making: A Model-Based Exploration Using Eye-Tracking Data," *Management Science* 59.5 (2013): 1009–26.

CHAPTER 4: THE NEW MIRROR

1. Avraham N. Kluger and Angelo DeNisi, "The Effects of Feedback Interventions on Performance: A Historical Review, a Meta-analysis, and a Preliminary Feedback Intervention Theory," *Psychological Bulletin* 119.2 (1996): 254.

2. Yaron Levi and Shlomo Benartzi, "Economic Behavior in the Digital Age," working paper, UCLA, 2014.

3. Board of Governors of the Federal Reserve System, "Consumers and Mobile Financial Services," 2014, http://www.federalreserve.gov/econ resdata/consumers-and-mobile-financial-services-report-201403.pdf.

4. James J. Choi, David Laibson, Brigitte C. Madrian, and Andrew Metrick, "Defined Contribution Pensions: Plan Rules, Participant Choices, and the Path of Least Resistance," in *Tax Policy and the Economy*, vol. 16, James Poterba, ed. (Cambridge, MA: MIT Press, 2002), 67–113.

5. See Dan Gardner and Philip Tetlock, "What's Wrong with Expert Predictions," *Cato Unbound*, July 11, 2011; also in Robin Hanson et al., *What's Wrong with Expert Predictions? (Cato Unbound)* (Cato Institute, Kindle Edition, 2011); Philip Tetlock, *Expert Political Judgment: How Good Is It? How Can We Know?* (Princeton University Press, 2005).

6. Tetlock, *Expert Political Judgment*.

7. Gardner and Tetlock, "What's Wrong with Expert Predictions."

8. http://www.doncio.navy.mil/chips/ArticleDetails.aspx?ID=5976.

9. Philip Tetlock and Dan Gardner, "Who's Good at Forecasts?" *The Economist*, October 31, 2013; Barbara Mellers, Eric Stone, Terny Murray, Angela Minster, Nick Rohrbaugh, Michael Bishop, Eva Chen, et al., "Identifying and Cultivating Superforecasters as a

Method of Improving Probabilistic Predictions," *Perspectives on Psychological Science* 10.3 (2015): 267–81.

10. Gardner and Tetlock, "What's Wrong with Expert Predictions."

11. Shlomo Benartzi and Richard H. Thaler, "Myopic Loss Aversion and the Equity Premium Puzzle," *The Quarterly Journal of Economics* 110.1 (1995): 73–92.

12. I owe a big thank-you to Yaron Levi for calculating these figures, based on an analysis of the data from 1926 to 2013.

13. Richard H. Thaler, Amos Tversky, Daniel Kahneman, and Alan Schwartz, "The Effect of Myopia and Loss Aversion on Risk Taking: An Experimental Test," *The Quarterly Journal of Economics* (1997): 647–61.

14. Benartzi and Thaler, "Myopic Loss Aversion and the Equity Premium Puzzle."

15. Benedetto De Martino, John P. O'Doherty, Debajyoti Ray, Peter Bossaerts, and Colin Camerer, "In the Mind of the Market: Theory of Mind Biases Value Computation During Financial Bubbles," *Neuron* 79.6 (2013): 1222–31.

16. http://www.caltech.edu/content/what-causes-some-participate -bubble-markets.

17. Terry Lohrenz, Meghana Bhatt, Nathan Apple, and P. Read Montague, "Keeping Up with the Joneses: Interpersonal Prediction Errors and the Correlation of Behavior in a Tandem Sequential Choice Task," *PLOS Computational Biology* 9.10 (2013): e1003275.

18. Maya Shaton, "The Display of Information and Household Investment Behavior," working paper, University of Chicago, 2014.

19. Solomon E. Asch, "Effects of Group Pressure upon the Modification and Distortion of Judgments," *Groups, Leadership, and Men* (1951): 222–36.

20. Christian Hildebrand, Andreas Herrmann, Gerald Häubl, and Jan R. Landwehr, "When Social Media Can Be Bad for You: Community

Feedback Stifles Consumer Creativity and Reduces Satisfaction with Self-Designed Products," *Information Systems Research* 24.1 (2013): 14–29.

21. Christian Hildebrand, Andreas Herrmann, Gerald Häubl, and Jan R. Landwehr, "Conformity and the Crowd," *Harvard Business Review* (July–August 2013): 23.

22. Adam Joinson, "Online Disinhibition," in Jayne Gackenbach, ed., *Psychology and the Internet: Intrapersonal, Interpersonal, and Transpersonal Implications* (Waltham, MA: Academic Press, 2011), chap. 4, 76–90.

23. http://hechingerreport.org/content/robo-readers-arent-good-human -readers-theyre-better_17021/.

24. Joinson, "Online Disinhibition."

25. http://home.isr.umich.edu/releases/texting-ups-truthfulness-new -iphone-study-suggests/.

26. Mandy Stahre, Jim Roeber, Dafna Kanny, and Robert D. Brewer, "Contribution of Excessive Alcohol Consumption to Deaths and Years of Potential Life Lost in the United States," *Preventing Chronic Disease* 11 (2014).

27. Philip J. Cook, *Paying the Tab: The Costs and Benefits of Alcohol Control* (Princeton, NJ: Princeton University Press, 2007).

28. http://www.washingtonpost.com/blogs/wonkblog/wp/2014/09/25/ think-you-drink-a-lot-this-chart-will-tell-you/.

29. Laura H. Lind, Michael F. Schober, Frederick G. Conrad, and Heidi Reichert, "Why Do Survey Respondents Disclose More When Computers Ask the Questions?" *Public Opinion Quarterly* 77(4) (2013): 888–935.

30. Kevin Coe, Kate Kenski, and Stephen A. Rains, "Online and Uncivil? Patterns and Determinants of Incivility in Newspaper Website Comments," *Journal of Communication* (2014).

31. http://www.businessinsider.com/tablets-are-making-waiters-obsolete -2014-6.

32. Avi Goldfarb, Ryan C. McDevitt, Sampsa Samila, and Brian Silverman, "The Effect of Social Interaction on Economic Transactions: Evidence from Changes in Two Retail Formats," *Management Science*, working paper, March 2015.

33. Janet Polivy, C. Peter Herman, Rick Hackett, and Irka Kuleshnyk, "The Effects of Self-Attention and Public Attention on Eating in Restrained and Unrestrained Subjects," *Journal of Personality and Social Psychology* 50.6 (1986): 1253.

34. http://www.latimes.com/books/jacketcopy/la-et-jc-fifty-shades-of -grey-tops-100-million-in-worldwide-sales-20140226-story.html.

35. http://socialtimes.com/50-shades-of-grey-is-selling-6x-more-kindle -books-than-print_b172674?red=en.

36. Daniel Fernandes, John G. Lynch Jr., and Richard G. Netemeyer, "Financial Literacy, Financial Education, and Downstream Financial Behaviors," *Management Science* 60.8 (August 2014): 1861–83.

37. http://www.thedailybeast.com/articles/2014/07/14/the-israeli-app -red-alert-saves-lives-but-it-just-might-drive-you-nuts.html.

38. Paul Slovic, Melissa Finucane, Ellen Peters, and Donald G. MacGregor, "The Affect Heuristic," in Thomas Gilovich, Dale Griffin, and Daniel Kahneman, eds., *Heuristics and Biases: The Psychology of Intuitive Judgment* (New York: Cambridge University Press, 2002), 397–420.

39. Julie Downs, George Loewenstein, and Jessica Wisdom, "Strategies for Promoting Healthier Food Choices," *American Economic Review* 99.2 (2009): 1–10.

40. Brian Elbel, Rogan Kersh, Victoria L. Brescoll, and L. Beth Dixon, "Calorie Labeling and Food Choices: A First Look at the Effects on Low-Income People in New York City," *Health Affairs* 28.6 (2009): w1110–w1121.

41. Etienne Vermeire, Hilary Hearnshaw, Paul Van Royen, and Joke Denekens, "Patient Adherence to Treatment: Three Decades of

Research. A Comprehensive Review," *Journal of Clinical Pharmacy and Therapeutics* 26.5 (2001): 331–42.

42. Ibid.

43. http://www.glowcaps.com.

44. https://www.google.com/patents/US20070016443.

45. http://www.vitality.net/research_harvard.html.

46. http://www.thedailybeast.com/articles/2014/07/14/the-israeli-app -red-alert-saves-lives-but-it-just-might-drive-you-nuts.html.

47. David W. Nickerson and Todd Rogers, "Do You Have a Voting Plan? Implementation Intentions, Voter Turnout, and Organic Plan Making," *Psychological Science* 21.2 (2010): 194–99.

48. Ayelet Fishbach, Tal Eyal, and Stacey R. Finkelstein, "How Positive and Negative Feedback Motivate Goal Pursuit," *Social and Personality Psychology Compass* 4.8 (2010): 517–30.

49. K. C. Diwas, Bradley R. Staats, and Francesca Gino, "Learning from My Success and from Others' Failure: Evidence from Minimally Invasive Cardiac Surgery," *Management Science* 59.11 (2013): 2435–49.

CHAPTER 5: DESIRABLE DIFFICULTY

1. Susan M. Belmore, "Reading Computer-Presented Text," *Bulletin of the Psychonomic Society* (1985).

2. John D. Gould, Lizette Alfaro, Vincent Barnes, Rich Finn, Nancy Grischkowsky, and Angela Minuto, "Reading Is Slower from CRT Displays Than from Paper: Attempts to Isolate a Single Variable Explanation," *Human Factors* 29(3) (1987): 269–99; J. D. Gould et al., "Reading from CRT Displays Can Be as Fast as Reading from Paper," *Human Factors* 29(5) (1987): 497–517; John D. Gould, Lizette Alfaro, Rich Finn, Brian Haupt, and Angela Minuto, "Why Is Reading Slower from CRT Displays Than from Paper," *Proceedings of*

the Human Factors and Ergonomics Society Annual Meeting 30.8 (SAGE Publications, 1986): 834–36.

3. Andrew Dillon, "Reading from Paper Versus Screens: A Critical Review of the Empirical Literature," *Ergonomics* 35.10 (1992): 1297–1326.

4. http://thingsofinterest.com/2014/10/22/difference-30-years-makes -imac-retina-5k-display-vs-original-macintosh/.

5. Anne Mangen, Bente R. Walgermo, and Kolbjørn Brønnick, "Reading Linear Texts on Paper Versus Computer Screen: Effects on Reading Comprehension," *International Journal of Educational Research* 58 (2013): 61–68.

6. In a largely neglected paper, Gould demonstrated that a 1986 IBM monitor using the 5080 graphics system—it had a 60Hz refresh rate and much higher resolution—was capable of erasing the screen reading gap. For the first time ever, readers using this display were able to read with the same speed and comprehension levels as those reading on paper. What explains this result? One intriguing possibility is that the 5080 represented a sweet spot of clarity. It was far easier to read than the previous generation of monochrome displays, but it wasn't too easy. John D. Gould et al., "Reading from CRT Displays Can Be as Fast as Reading from Paper," *Human Factors: The Journal of the Human Factors and Ergonomics Society* 29.5 (1987): 497–517.

7. http://www.mckinsey.com/insights/public_sector/nudging_the_world _toward_smarter_public_policy_an_interview_with_richard_thaler.

8. http://www.transactionworld.net/articles/2013/november/ mcommerce.html.

9. United States, Executive Office of the President and National Economic Council, "Simplifying Student Aid: The Case for an Easier, Faster, and More Accurate FAFSA" (September 2009), retrieved from http://www.whitehouse.gov/assets/documents/FAFSA_Report.pdf.

10. Connor Diemand-Yauman, Daniel M. Oppenheimer, and Erikka B. Vaughan, "Fortune Favors the **Bold** (*and the Italicized*): Effects of Disfluency on Educational Outcomes," *Cognition* 118.1 (2011): 111–15.

11. Shane Frederick, "Cognitive Reflection and Decision Making," *Journal of Economic Perspectives* (2005): 25–42.

12. Adam Alter, Daniel M. Oppenheimer, Nicholas Epley, and Rebecca N. Eyre, "Overcoming Intuition: Metacognitive Difficulty Activates Analytic Reasoning," *Journal of Experimental Psychology: General* 136.4 (2007): 569.

13. Andrew Meyer, Shane Frederick, Terence C. Burnham, Juan D. Guevara Pinto, Ty W. Boyer, Linden J. Ball, Gordon Pennycook, et al., "Disfluent Fonts Don't Help People Solve Math Problems," *Journal of Experimental Psychology: General* 144.2 (2015): e16.

14. Adam L. Alter, Daniel M. Oppenheimer, Nicholas Epley, and Rebecca N. Eyre, "Overcoming Intuition: Metacognitive Difficulty Activates Analytic Reasoning," *Journal of Experimental Psychology: General* 136.4 (2007): 569.

15. http://edge.org/conversation/disfluency.

16. https://www.federalregister.gov/articles/2013/12/31/2013-28210/integrated-mortgage-disclosures-under-the-real-estate-settlement-procedures-act-regulation-x-and-the.

17. Pam A. Mueller and Daniel M. Oppenheimer, "The Pen Is Mightier Than the Keyboard: Advantages of Longhand over Laptop Note Taking," *Psychological Science* 25.6 (June 2014): 1159–68.

18. Linda Henkel, "Point-and-Shoot Memories: The Influence of Taking Photos on Memory for a Museum Tour," *Psychological Science* 25.2 (February 2014): 396–402.

19. http://www.psychologicalscience.org/index.php/news/releases/no-pictures-please-taking-photos-may-impede-memory-of-museum-tour.html.

20. Brian Reimer, Bruce Mehler, Jonathan Dobres, Joseph F. Coughlin, Steve Matteson, David Gould, Nadine Chanine, and Vladimir Levantovsky, "Assessing the Impact of Typeface Design in a Text-Rich Automotive User Interface," *Ergonomics* (2014): 1–16.

21. http://www.igmchicago.org/igm-economic-experts-panel/poll
    -results?SurveyID=SV_eyDrhnya7vAPrX7.

22. https://support.uber.com/hc/en-us/articles/201836656-What-is
    -surge-pricing-and-how-does-it-work; http://www.businessinsider
    .com/uber-new-years-eve-surge-pricing-2014-1.

CHAPTER 6: DIGITAL TAILORING

1. David B. Strohmetz, Bruce Rind, Reed Fisher, and Michael Lynn, "Sweetening the Till: The Use of Candy to Increase Restaurant Tipping," *Journal of Applied Social Psychology* 32.2 (2002): 300–309.

2. Diana I. Cordova and Mark R. Lepper, "Intrinsic Motivation and the Process of Learning: Beneficial Effects of Contextualization, Personalization, and Choice," *Journal of Educational Psychology* 88.4 (1996): 715.

3. Noah J. Goldstein, Robert B. Cialdini, and Vladas Griskevicius, "A Room with a Viewpoint: Using Social Norms to Motivate Environmental Conservation in Hotels," *Journal of Consumer Research* 35.3 (2008): 472–82.

4. Ibid.

5. http://www.coca-colacompany.com/innovation/your-name-in-lights
    -personalized-coke-billboards-greet-consumers-in-israel.

6. http://www.seeplatform.eu/casestudies/Behavioural%20Insights%
    20Team.

7. Thank you to Michael Hallsworth of the Behavioural Insights Team for sharing the study results.

8. Hal E. Hershfield et al., "Increasing Saving Behavior Through Age-Progressed Renderings of the Future Self," *Journal of Marketing Research* 48.SPL (2011): S23–S37.

9. Ibid.; Hal Ersner-Hershfield, G. Elliott Wimmer, and Brian Knutson, "Saving for the Future Self: Neural Measures of Future Self-Continuity Predict Temporal Discounting," *Social Cognitive and Affective Neuroscience* 4.1 (2009): 85–92.

10. James J. Choi, David Laibson, Brigitte C. Madrian, and Andrew Metrick, "Defined Contribution Pensions: Plan Rules, Participant Choices, and the Path of Least Resistance," in *Tax Policy and the Economy*, vol. 16, James Poterba, ed. (Cambridge, MA: MIT Press, 2002), 67–113.

11. Danny Kalish, telephone interview, March 11, 2014.

12. idomoo.com, "Annual Utility Statement," http://idomoo.com/video/annual-utility-statement.html.

13. Hengchen Dai, Katherine L. Milkman, and Jason Riis, "The Fresh Start Effect: Temporal Landmarks Motivate Aspirational Behavior," *Management Science* 60.10 (2014): 2563–82.

14. Michael Sanders and Michael Hallsworth, "Applying Behavioural Economics in a Health Policy Context: Dispatches from the Front Lines," in *Behavioral Economics and Public Health*, Christina A. Roberto and Ichiro Kawachi, eds. (New York: Oxford University Press, 2015).

15. Many thanks to Michael Hallsworth of the Behavioural Insights Team for sharing the data.

16. http://kb.mailchimp.com/article/when-is-the-best-time-to-send-emails/; https://econsultancy.com/blog/62688-six-case-studies-and-infographics-on-the-optimal-time-to-send-emails#i.1ydxjvz138deen.

17. Daniel Fernandes, John G. Lynch Jr., and Richard G. Netemeyer, "Financial Literacy, Financial Education, and Downstream Financial Behaviors," *Management Science* 60.8 (August 2014): 1861–83.

18. http://www.forbes.com/sites/onmarketing/2014/01/29/yes-a-super-bowl-ad-really-is-worth-4-million/.

19. https://www.gov.uk/government/uploads/system/uploads/attachment_data/file/83719/Behavioural-Insights-Team-Annual-Update-2011-12_0.pdf.

20. Shlomo Benartzi, "Nudging Brits to Do the Right Things," interview with Dr. David Halpern, *Psychology and Personal Finance*, October 8, 2013, http://www.anderson.ucla.edu/faculty/accounting/faculty/psychology-and-personal-finance.

CHAPTER 7: THE CHOICE OPPORTUNITY

1. http://thehill.com/policy/healthcare/328797-analysis-less
   -than-1-percent-of-users-initially-enrolled-at-healthcaregov.

2. This figure is based on accessing healthcare.gov during the 2014
   open enrollment period.

3. George Loewenstein, Joelle Y. Friedman, Barbara McGill, Sarah
   Ahmad, Suzanne Linck, Stacey Sinkula, John Beshears, et al.,
   "Consumers' Misunderstanding of Health Insurance," *Journal of
   Health Economics* 32.5 (2013): 850–62.

4. It's worth pointing out that the precise numbers of online products
   are in constant flux, depending on who is searching and when. In the
   time I've been writing this chapter, the number of men's shoes
   available on Zappos has fluctuated between roughly fifteen thousand
   and seventeen thousand options.

5. Adam M. Grant and Barry Schwartz, "Too Much of a Good Thing:
   The Challenge and Opportunity of the Inverted U," *Perspectives on
   Psychological Science* 6.1 (2011): 61–76.

6. Avni M. Shah and George Wolford, "Buying Behavior as a Function
   of Parametric Variation of Number of Choices," *Psychological Science*
   18.5 (2007): 369–70.

7. Sheena S. Iyengar and Mark R. Lepper, "When Choice Is
   Demotivating: Can One Desire Too Much of a Good Thing?"
   Journal of Personality and Social Psychology 79.6 (2000): 995.

8. Sheena S. Iyengar, Gur Huberman, and Wei Jiang, "How Much Choice
   Is Too Much? Contributions to 401(k) Retirement Plans," in *Pension
   Design and Structure: New Lessons from Behavioral Finance*, eds. Olivia
   Mitchell and Stephen Utkus (New York: Oxford University Press, 2004),
   83–95.

9. Justin Beneke, Alice Cumming, and Lindsey Jolly, "The Effect of
   Item Reduction on Assortment Satisfaction—A Consideration of the
   Category of Red Wine in a Controlled Retail Setting," *Journal of
   Retailing and Consumer Services* 20.3 (2013): 282–91.

10. Tom MacNeil, in-person interview, July 29, 2014.

11. John A. Howard and Jagdish N. Sheth, *The Theory of Buyer Behavior* (New York: Wiley, 1969).

12. John R. Hauser and Birger Wernerfelt, "An Evaluation Cost Model of Consideration Sets," *Journal of Consumer Research* (1990): 393–408.

13. Cassie Mogilner, Tamar Rudnick, and Sheena S. Iyengar, "The Mere Categorization Effect: How the Presence of Categories Increases Choosers' Perceptions of Assortment Variety and Outcome Satisfaction," *Journal of Consumer Research* 35.2 (2008): 202–15.

14. Jeffrey R. Parker and Donald R. Lehmann, "How and When Grouping Low-Calorie Options Reduces the Benefits of Providing Dish-Specific Calorie Information," *Journal of Consumer Research* 41.1 (2014): 213–35.

15. Mogilner, Rudnick, and Iyengar, "The Mere Categorization Effect."

16. Itamar Simonson and Emanuel Rosen, "Three Long-Held Concepts Every Marketer should Rethink," *Harvard Business Review* (January 2014).

17. http://blogs.ft.com/tech-blog/2014/03/why-the-music-industrys-fat -head-is-eating-its-long-tail/.

18. Joshua Porter, "Testing the Three-Click Rule," *User Interface Engineering* (April 16, 2003), http://www.uie.com/articles/three_ click_rule/.

19. http://www.smithsonianmag.com/history/a-brief-history-of- wimbledon-156205892/?no-ist; http://www.history.com/this- day-in-history/wimbledon-tournament-begins; http://www. wimbledon.com/en_GB/history/index.html.

20. http://www.wimbledon.com/en_GB/history/index.html; http://en.wikipedia.org/wiki/The_Championships,_Wimbledon.

21. Tibor Besedes, Cary Deck, Sudipta Sarangi, and Mikhael Shor, "Reducing Choice Overload Without Reducing Choices," *Review of Economics and Statistics*, forthcoming.

22. Tibor Besedes, telephone interview, May 29, 2014.

23. http://www.nyc.gov/html/housinginfo/html/apartments/apartment
    _hunting_tips.shtml.

24. Iyengar and Lepper, "When Choice Is Demotivating."

25. Yangjie Gu, Simona Botti, and David Faro, "Turning the Page: The
    Impact of Choice Closure on Satisfaction," *Journal of Consumer
    Research* 40.2 (2013): 268–83.

26. David Faro, telephone interview, June 3, 2014.

27. Yangjie Gu, Simona Botti, and David Faro, "Seeking and
    Avoiding Choice Closure," working paper, London Business
    School, 2014.

28. http://www.bls.gov/news.release/cesan.nr0.htm.

29. Saurabh Bhargava, George Loewenstein, and Justin Sydnor. "Choose to
    Lose? Employee Health-Plan Decisions from a Menu with Dominated
    Options," working paper, Carnegie Mellon University, 2014.

30. Loewenstein et al., "Consumers' Misunderstanding of Health
    Insurance," 850–62.

31. Saurabh Bhargava et al., "Choose to Lose?"

32. Jason Abaluck and Jonathan Gruber, "Heterogeneity in Choice
    Inconsistencies Among the Elderly: Evidence from Prescription
    Drug Plan Choice," *The American Economic Review* 101.3 (2011):
    377–81.

33. Peter A. Ubel, David A. Comerford, and Eric Johnson, "Healthcare
    .gov 3.0—Behavioral Economics and Insurance Exchanges," *New
    England Journal of Medicine* 372.8 (2015): 695–98.

34. http://aspe.hhs.gov/health/reports/2014/Premiums/
    2014MktPlacePremBrf.pdf, p. 10.

35. Itamar Simonson and Amos Tversky, "Choice in Context: Tradeoff
    Contrast and Extremeness Aversion," *Journal of Marketing Research* (1992).

CHAPTER 8: THINKING ARCHITECTURE

1. http://www.imshealth.com/deployedfiles/imshealth/Global/Content
   /Corporate/IMS%20Health%20Institute/Reports/Patient_Apps/
   IIHI_Patient_Apps_Report.pdf.

2. James J. Choi, David Laibson, Brigitte C. Madrian, and Andrew Metrick, "Defined Contribution Pensions: Plan Rules, Participant Choices, and the Path of Least Resistance," in *Tax Policy and the Economy*, vol. 16, James Poterba, ed. (Cambridge, MA: MIT Press, 2002) 67–113.

3. Alicia Munnell, "Falling Short: The Coming Retirement Crisis and What to Do About It," Center for Retirement Research at Boston College, April 2015.

4. http://www.scientificamerican.com/article/how-mobile-phones-can
   -solve-the-retirement-crisis/.

5. Eric J. Johnson, Gerald Häubl, and Anat Keinan, "Aspects of Endowment: A Query Theory of Value Construction," *Journal of Experimental Psychology: Learning, Memory, and Cognition* 33.3 (2007): 461.

6. David J. Hardisty, Eric J. Johnson, and Elke U. Weber, "A Dirty Word or a Dirty World? Attribute Framing, Political Affiliation, and Query Theory," *Psychological Science* 21.1 (2010): 86–92.

7. https://www.gov.uk/government/uploads/system/uploads/
   attachment_data/file/267100/Applying_Behavioural_Insights_to
   _Organ_Donation.pdf.

8. Elke U. Weber, Eric J. Johnson, Kerry F. Milch, Hannah Chang, Jeffrey C. Brodscholl, and Daniel G. Goldstein, "Asymmetric Discounting in Intertemporal Choice a Query-Theory Account," *Psychological Science* 18.6 (2007): 516–23.

9. David Romer, "Do Firms Maximize? Evidence from Professional Football," *Journal of Political Economy* 114.2 (2006): 340–65.

10. Daniel Kahneman and Amos Tversky, "Prospect Theory: An Analysis of Decision Under Risk," *Econometrica: Journal of the Econometric Society* (1979): 263–91.

11. http://www.coldhardfootballfacts.com/content/nfl-coaches-are
-more-gutless-than-ever-fourth-down/19370/.

12. David Faro and Yuval Rottenstreich, "Affect, Empathy, and
Regressive Mispredictions of Others' Preferences Under Risk,"
Management Science 52.4 (2006): 529–41.

13. Timothy D. Wilson, David A. Reinhard, Erin C. Westgate, Daniel
T. Gilbert, Nicole Ellerbeck, Cheryl Hahn, Casey L. Brown, and Adi
Shared, "Just Think: The Challenges of the Disengaged Mind,"
Science 345.6192 (2014): 75–77.

14. Shlomo Benartzi and Roger Lewin, *Seven Steps to Your Fulfilling
Retirement . . . and Life* (New York: Portfolio, 2015).

15. Samuel D. Bond, Kurt A. Carlson, and Ralph L. Keeney,
"Generating Objectives: Can Decision Makers Articulate What
They Want?" *Management Science* 54.1 (2008): 56–70.

INDEX